T0083866

AN EXHIBITION

IN COMMEMORATION

OF THE

HUNDREDTH ANNIVERSARY

OF THE DEATH OF

LEWIS CARROLL

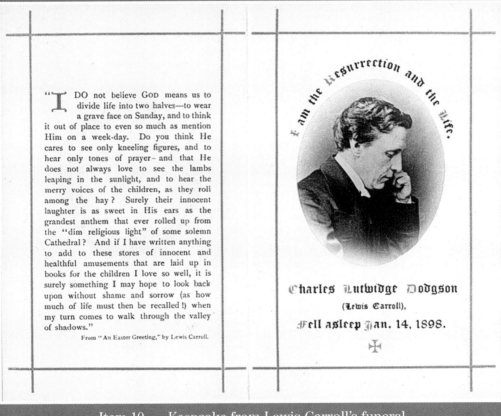

"I DO not believe GOD means us to divide life into two halves—to wear a grave face on Sunday, and to think it out of place to even so much as mention Him on a week-day. Do you think He cares to see only kneeling figures, and to hear only tones of prayer—and that He does not always love to see the lambs leaping in the sunlight, and to hear the merry voices of the children, as they roll among the hay? Surely their innocent laughter is as sweet in His ears as the grandest anthem that ever rolled up from the "dim religious light" of some solemn Cathedral? And if I have written anything to add to these stores of innocent and healthful amusements that are laid up in books for the children I love so well, it is surely something I may hope to look back upon without shame and sorrow (as how much of life must then be recalled!) when my turn comes to walk through the valley of shadows."

From "An Easter Greeting," by Lewis Carroll.

I am the Resurrection and the Life.

Charles Lutwidge Dodgson
(Lewis Carroll),
Fell asleep Jan. 14, 1898.

Item 10   Keepsake from Lewis Carroll's funeral.

yours very sincerely
C. L. Dodgson
(alias "Lewis Carroll".)

AN EXHIBITION FROM

THE

JON A. LINDSETH COLLECTION

OF

C. L. DODGSON AND LEWIS CARROLL

ON VIEW AT

THE GROLIER CLUB

APRIL 1 THROUGH MAY 29, 1998

THE GROLIER CLUB

NEW YORK

1998

ISBN 0-910672-23-7

The Grolier Club
47 East 60th Street
New York, NY 10022

To William Self
who knows great books

CONTENTS

		Page
	Acknowledgments	10
	Introduction	11
I	*C. L. Dodgson (alias "Lewis Carroll")* by Edward Guiliano	17
II	*The 1865 Alice* by Selwyn H. Goodacre	29
III	*Sir John Tenniel and Lewis Carroll* by Rodney Engen	35
IV	*Charles L. Dodgson, Mathematician* by Francine F. Abeles	45
V	*Lewis Carroll's Photography* by Edward Wakeling	55
VI	*"Are You Kissable?"* by Morton N. Cohen	68
VII	*Lewis Carroll, Bibliophile* by Jeffrey Stern	75
VIII	*"An inscribed book is 54.37 as valuable to me...."* by Jon A. Lindseth	81
IX	*Lewis Carroll, Pre-Raphaelitism and Christina Rossetti* by Jeffrey Stern	89
X	*Charles L. Dodgson and the Theater* by Charles C. Lovett	103
XI	*Lewis Carroll Comes to America* by Selwyn H. Goodacre	113
XII	*Alice in Translation* by Jon A. Lindseth	123
	The Lewis Carroll Society	125
	Notes on Contributors	126
	Colophon	127

ACKNOWLEDGMENTS

In the Lewis Carroll world there is an active support network of like-minded people. This network includes the members of the several Lewis Carroll Societies and the many booksellers who deal in Carroll material. A special mention is due to Stephen Rudin who assembled and then sold me his fine Carroll collection, strong in letters and photographs, and to Kevin MacDonnell for finding the "twilight version" of *Merryman's Monthly,* the only known copy. Within the past year, William Self sold me his 1865 *Alice,* one of the great rarities of the book world, and for this I am extremely grateful. These are just three examples of help received in developing this collection; there have been many others.

To the essay writers for this catalogue, my particular thanks. Each has expertise in his or her field and the willingness of each to contribute is greatly appreciated. My thanks to Morton Cohen, the distinguished dean of Carroll scholars, for his enormous contribution to the Carroll world and to this catalogue. Thanks to Selwyn Goodacre who wrote two essays, to Edward Wakeling, to Francine Abeles, to Edward Guiliano, to Charles Lovett and to Rodney Engen. Jeffrey Stern wrote two essays and helped in many other ways.

At The Grolier Club, Mary Schlosser, Chair of the Small Exhibitions Committee; Carol Rothkopf, Chair of the Publications Committee; Nancy Houghton and Eric Holzenberg, were all very helpful.

The Berg Collection of English and American Literature, The New York Public Library, Astor, Lenox and Tilden Foundations, was kind to loan *The Children's Library,* the only known copy, so that for the first time, the three Jesse Haney piracies of *Alice's Adventures in Wonderland* could be displayed together.

Linda Mayer entered this catalogue in the computer and assisted in proofreading. The entire typescript was read by Bea Sidaway, and was read in part by Virginia Lindseth, Morton Cohen, Edward Wakeling and Jeffrey Stern. Carol Rothkopf edited this catalogue with conviction and compassion. To each my thanks. What errors remain are mine.

Assistance with this catalogue was also received from Joel Birenbaum, Justin Schiller and Jay Dillon.

Thanks to my long-time associate and fellow Carroll enthusiast, Bea Sidaway, for her years of intelligent and energetic work, not only on this catalogue and exhibition but on so many other Carroll projects as well. Bea has catalogued over 3,000 Carroll items in a complete computer data base. She has traveled to California to inventory and pack Carroll material, and she inventoried and packed a collection of duplicates for Japan. She is in constant E-mail communication with a number of Carroll scholars and with many libraries. Her developing census of inscribed copies of the first edition of *Through the Looking-Glass* is eagerly awaited. I am forever grateful to her.

J. A. L.

INTRODUCTION

April 1, 1998, is a fitting day to open an exhibition that commemorates the centennial of Lewis Carroll's death. In a letter to his publisher, Macmillan, Carroll asked that his nonsense poem, *The Hunting of the Snark*, be published this day in 1876. He wrote: "Please take a memorandum to advertise the *Snark* 'to be published on the 1st of April.' Surely that is the fittest day for it to appear?"

Carroll was indeed concerned that by appearing on April Fool's Day his book would not be taken seriously. But, later, when he was asked about the poem's meaning, Carroll could only say: "I'm very much afraid I didn't mean anything but nonsense!"

In the same year in which the *Snark* was published, Harcourt Amory graduated from Harvard and he began to assemble the first great Carroll collection, now in the Harvard College Library. Since then, interest in Carroll's work by collectors, biographers and critics of all persuasions has been constant.

In Lewis Carroll's obituary in *The Times* (London) of January 15, 1898, one reads:

> It is curious to notice how frequently *Alice in Wonderland* is quoted in reference to public affairs, as well as to ordinary matters of every day life. Hardly a week passes without the employment of its whimsicalities to point a moral or adorn a tale.

To find out just how often "the employment of its whimsicalities" occurs in American newspapers and magazines, I engaged Bacon's news clipping service to clip all citations of both Lewis Carroll and *Alice's Adventures in Wonderland* for a six-month period, from June to November 1991. What I found was 2,074 citations for the period, more than eleven each day, in the United States alone.

Here are some citations from *The New York Times*:

- A theater review: "The eccentricity is like an *Alice in Wonderland* inversion of reality."
- An inner city school story: "One feels as if one had slipped, *Alice in Wonderland*-like, into some fictional space."
- About a bird sanctuary: "We cherish *Alice in Wonderland* memories."
- A Mobil Oil Op-Ed ad: "If Lewis Carroll's little Alice were wandering the halls of Congress, she would certainly find some things 'curiouser and curiouser.'"
- A story on the drug problem entitled: *"Misadventures in Cocaland."*
- A story on California's move to force insurers to make policy rebates: "The plan amounts to 35 pages of *Alice in Wonderland* regulations."

How often do other authors or literary classics receive this kind of attention in the press? I do not have survey data, but other than the Bible and Shakespeare, I would expect to find very few, if any, that could match the number of references to Lewis Carroll and *Alice*.

In the *School Library Journal* of March 1977, Alleen Pace Nilsen, reporting on her study of the influence of children's literature on the language of the mass media, wrote: "Of the longer pieces of literature, the one most often referred to was Lewis Carroll's *Alice in Wonderland* and its companion *Through the Looking-Glass.*"

So, while in popular culture Carroll is of interest because of the "whimsicalities" of his *Alice* books, to collectors and critics it is the complexity of the man, his genius in all that he accomplished, that captures us.

Charles Lutwidge Dodgson was born January 27, 1832, at Daresbury, Cheshire, and died January 14, 1898, at the home of his sisters in Guildford, Surrey. He was educated at home until age 12, when he entered Richmond School, after which he went to Rugby. He matriculated at Christ Church, Oxford, in 1850, where he would spend the rest of his life. His father had earned a rare double first honors at Christ Church, and the younger Charles Dodgson would later earn a first – his in mathematics.

In December 1852, he was nominated a Student of Christ Church, an appointment to which two conditions were attached: he should remain unmarried and he should proceed to Holy Orders. With the appointment as Student he received life tenure and rooms. In 1856, he was appointed Mathematical Lecturer and that same year he published his first work using the pseudonym, *Lewis Carroll.* That poem, "Solitude," was published in *The Train: A First-Class Magazine*, a copy of which is included in this exhibition.

He received a Master of Arts in 1857, and in 1861 was ordained deacon. He resigned his mathematics lectureship in 1881 but accepted other college assignments until his death.

Charles Dodgson (alias "Lewis Carroll") is best known for *Alice's Adventures in Wonderland,* a story he first published in 1865, and the sequel *Through the Looking-Glass*, which appeared in 1872. Edward Guiliano charts Dodgson's use of the Lewis Carroll pseudonym in his essay, the first in this catalogue. In the eleven essays that follow, the authors explore other interests and work of Lewis Carroll.

Opportunities to collect Carrolliana are vast. Carroll published over 300 works during his lifetime and took some 3,000 photographs. In addition, his letter register contained over 98,000 entries. Translations of his books exceed 2,000 different editions and printings, and parodies of *Alice* probably add up to 500 or more. Illustrators of English language editions of *Alice* exceed 250 and a decent reference library for a Carroll scholar might contain as many as 500 works. Thus, while this exhibition covers a broad range of Carroll's writing and interests, it is also notable for what is omitted, including:

- Verse. Carroll loved to write poetry and did so in much of his work. The best book on this subject is *The Collected Verse of Lewis Carroll* published by Macmillan in 1933. A great deal has been found since then, but much scholarly work still needs to be done.

- Games and Puzzles. The creation of puzzles and games was one of Carroll's chief interests as can be seen by the large number of books and pamphlets he published on the subject. He included games and puzzles in journal articles and in his letters. Books have been written about this aspect of Carroll's work; assembled, his puzzles would make a fascinating separate exhibition.

- <u>Public Affairs</u>. Carroll was interested in the issues of the times, and he frequently wrote about them in pamphlets, periodicals and letters to editors. How his thinking and writing on public affairs evolved has never been analyzed in depth and deserves scholarly attention.

- <u>Parodies</u>. Carroll parodied many writers, including Tennyson, Wordsworth, Coleridge, Charles Lamb, Isaac Watts and Longfellow. And, in turn, Carroll's *Alice* has been parodied hundreds of times, over 300 of which are in my collection. Little scholarly work has been done in this area.

- <u>Merchandise</u>. Lewis Carroll remains a potent cultural force in the world a hundred years after his death. An examination of the use of *Alice* images on retail merchandise reveals just how powerful the force is. Alice must be a great salesman if the Walt Disney Company is any example. They use her image often, on everything from books to stickers, notepaper, wallets and marionettes. We find her image and that of the White Rabbit, the Hatter and others on Limoges plates, Royal Doulton mugs, wood toys, neckties, soap, playing cards, tea towels, cookies, paper dolls and an enormous list of other things. This is not a recent phenomenon. *Alice* merchandise started appearing during Carroll's lifetime. My collection includes sheet music from 1870, a print suitable for framing from 1875, lantern slides from about 1880, a "Birthday Book" of 1884 and a tea tin of about 1895. A scholar of cultural history would find fertile ground for research here.

Lewis Carroll caught the imagination of Americans early. The greatest library collections of his work are in this country, all but The University of Texas collection being in the Northeast. Many of these libraries will have Carroll exhibits this centennial year. The Morgan Library exhibition will be on view from May 22 to August 30, 1998, and other exhibits will be shown at Harvard, Princeton, New York University, and the Rosenbach Museum and Library. Texas will mount an exhibit and have a series of lectures over six weeks starting in October. In England there will be a full year of Carroll activity which started with a January 10, 1998, commemorative ceremony at Lewis Carroll's plaque in Poets' Corner, Westminster Abbey, and a dinner at Christ Church on January 14, the centennial of his death. From May 8 to 17, Guildford will hold ten days of celebration, and Oxford University will conduct a one-week conference on Carroll, opening August 16, 1998. This is Lewis Carroll's year.

Carroll followed the practice of the Roman poet Catullus in noting a very special day in his *Diary*. Just as we might refer to a "red letter day," he would write: "I mark this day with a white stone." He made twenty-six such *Diary* entries over a span of 36 years, from 1855 to 1891.

Lewis Carroll would, I think, be surprised but pleased with the world-wide interest in his life and work. At The Grolier Club, in commemoration of the centennial of his death, we mark this day with a "white stone."

Jon A. Lindseth

THE CATALOGUE
WITH 114 ILLUSTRATIONS

"and what is the use of a book,"
thought Alice, "without pictures...?"
Alice's Adventures in Wonderland, Chapter I

SOLITUDE.

BY LEWIS CARROLL.

I LOVE the stillness of the wood,
I love the music of the rill,
I love to couch in pensive mood
Upon some silent hill.

Far off, beneath yon arching trees,
The silver-crested ripples pass,
And, like a mimic brook, the breeze
Whispers among the grass.

Item 2   The first use of the pseudonym "Lewis Carroll."

I
C. L. Dodgson (alias "Lewis Carroll")

By Edward Guiliano

He referred to it variously as his alias, his "nom de plume," his pseudonym, but "Lewis Carroll" was more than a convenience to protect his privacy, it was a crucial persona and identity for the Reverend Charles Lutwidge Dodgson.

Dodgson, the eccentric, paradoxical, brilliant mathematician, logician, teacher, letter writer, poet, wit, photographer, stammerer who lost his stammer in the company of children, and troubled, yet fascinating, Victorian, became universally known as Lewis Carroll. He created a work and character more famous than its author, and a pen name more famous than his own name and among the most well-known in literature.

It was not unusual among the Victorians to use pen names, and as a child Dodgson took to using a number of assumed initials to sign his juvenilia. For reasons unknown, he settled upon "B.B.," using it as one of six pseudonyms in *The Rectory Magazine*, which he wrote at age 16. He subsequently attached it to various story and verse contributions. The repetition and reverse appeal of B.B. struck his fancy for some reason – and 28 years later it is echoed in his choice of names for the crew in *The Hunting of the Snark*. The Bellman, Boots, a maker of Bonnets, a Barrister, a Broker, a Billiard-maker, a Banker, a Beaver all share, obviously, an initial letter B, as does a Boojum.

It was his boyhood pseudonymous identifier "B.B." that he attached to a set of submissions to *The Train*, a predominantly humorous monthly magazine published between 1856 and 1858 by Edmund Yates and his friends. It succeeded their defunct *Comic Times*, to which Dodgson had contributed. Yates, however, asked the 24 year-old Dodgson for a more suitable pseudonym. Dodgson first submitted "Dares," drawn from the name of the village where he was born, Daresbury. Yates found it "too much like a newspaper signature" and asked him to try again. Dodgson records in his *Diary*:

> *Feb: 11.* Wrote to Mr. Yates sending him a choice of names: 1. *Edgar Cuthwellis* (made by transposition out of 'Charles Lutwidge'). 2. *Edgar U. C. Westhill* (ditto). 3. *Louis Carroll*, (derived from Lutwidge = Ludovic = Louis, and Charles [Carolus]. 4. *Lewis Carroll*. (ditto).

A few days later, Yates fixed on Lewis Carroll. In March 1856, "Solitude," an unsophisticated romantic poem treating the recapturing of lost innocence and childhood, appeared in *The Train* signed Lewis Carroll.

From that first appearance of the Latinized reversal of his two first names, Charles Lutwidge, there is a pattern of authorship and identity in Dodgson's life and published works. His writings for children and his other humorous and recreational efforts, including many letters to his child-friends, are signed Lewis Carroll. His mathematical works, his serious letters and works relating especially to his duties at Christ Church are signed with his real name. A third signatory option he employed throughout his life was anonymity, sending off letters to publications, writing about Oxford internal affairs, or publishing little pieces on mathematics or logic intended for a small audience.

If he was confused about his own identity – and he was – the choice of name gave order to the parts of his personality. As Lewis Carroll he could tap deep springs of imagination and emotion outside the restraints of C. L. Dodgson. It was as Lewis Carroll that he told the story of Alice's adventures that "golden afternoon" to the Liddell sisters and signed his pen name to one of the most famous of all works of literature, a work in which questions of being and identity are never far from the reader.

"Who are you?" the Caterpillar asks Alice in a languid, sleepy voice at the start of Chapter V of *Alice's Adventures in Wonderland*. Unnerving transformation of body forms and size – from Alice's telescoping neck to a child that turns into a pig – figure prominently in the *Alice* books as do questions about life and death. Life as a dream motif, prominent in *Through the Looking-Glass*, rises to metaphysical status when Tweedledee challenges Alice about her existence in the Red King's dream: "And if he left off dreaming about you, where do you suppose you'd be?...You'd be nowhere. Why, you're only a sort of thing in his dream!"

"Who am I?" a standard issue of early childhood, was a dominant question in Dodgson's life, a question perhaps stimulated in his formative years when as the third child and first male, he was bracketed in roughly two-year intervals by two elder and by two younger sisters – strange, mysterious and different creatures for a young boy to contemplate. If one reads Dodgson's letters and diaries and studies his creative works, the theme of personal identity emerges throughout. He recognized himself as different, awkward, and at odds with what was manifest in other men and boys. He had doubts and fears and was haunted by guilt. He found some release or control for his pain, and perhaps his sexual energies, through order and discipline so characteristic of the Reverend Charles Dodgson but also through escape – escape into the world of Lewis Carroll.

His interest in and talent for photography can be seen as a variation on the theme of personal identity. "The black art," as photography was known, enabled the photographer to freeze time, fool death, and to attempt to capture the soul of a sitter. It is not by coincidence that Dodgson was predominantly a portrait photographer and that his frequent subjects were for him idealized subjects, young girls and famous people. Moreover, his fascination with change and identity extended to costume photography. What was he attempting when he dressed the young, upper-class Alice Liddell as a beggar-child in worn and torn clothes with her breast and nipple exposed? What was he imagining when he accumulated a costume wardrobe for photographing the young girls who were his child-friends and inspiration? At the surface level, he was indulging his theatrical impulses, which are also wedded to transformations and identity. For

Dodgson, these impulses dated back to his childhood when he wrote and directed some marionette plays, again a choice of play and amusement resonant with questions of being.

One of the curiosities of Dodgson's being is how diligently he worked at keeping his identities apart. No doubt the parade of children up to his rooms at Christ Church to be photographed and the hundreds of inscribed copies of his *Alice* books he sent to children made his identity an open secret at Oxford and among families of a certain class, but the shy don did not welcome his fame as Lewis Carroll. He did not sign autographs nor acknowledge to the general public that he was Lewis Carroll. He sent back letters addressed to Lewis Carroll at Christ Church unopened. He wrote to publications beseeching them not to connect Charles L. Dodgson with his pen name. In his letters, he repeatedly expressed his wish to avoid the mention of his real name in conjunction with Lewis Carroll and his works. He claimed he used the name "Lewis Carroll" in order to avoid all *personal* publicity and wished to be able to go unnoticed in public places.

However, he was not beyond using his books and identity as Lewis Carroll to gain an acquaintance with a young girl, and once the personal relationship grew, the open secret of his identity permitted him to move in and out of his identities with his child-friends, who were seemingly as at ease with this as he was. And because his pen name carried a certain stature well beyond that of a retiring Oxford don, he used it when writing about a cause he felt strongly about. Then again, he guarded his separate identities to preserve his reputation as a mathematician and serious thinker, not wanting professionals to dismiss these efforts arbitrarily as being from the author of *Alice's Adventures in Wonderland*.

His defense of this privacy and against the threatening fusion of the two men in one reached its foremost expression in 1890 when he had a leaflet, *The Stranger Circular*, printed:

> Mr. Dodgson is so frequently addressed by strangers on the quite unauthorized assumption that he claims, or at any rate acknowledges the authorship of books not published under his name, that he has found it necessary to print this, once for all, as an answer to all such applications. He neither claims nor acknowledges any connection with any pseudonym, or with any book that is not published under his own name. Having therefore no claim to retain, or even to read the enclosed, he returns it for the convenience of the writer who has thus misaddressed it.

He pursued this policy to his death, though the circle of friends who knew his dual identity grew. In the end, the names Lewis Carroll and Charles Lutwidge Dodgson were connected in print on a keepsake from his funeral [Item 10].

ITEMS EXHIBITED

1) **C. L. Dodgson (alias "Lewis Carroll") to Mrs. Jemima Rix.**
Autograph letter signed. March 9, 1885.

This letter signed "C. L. Dodgson (alias 'Lewis Carroll')" is a rare but not unique instance of Dodgson penning both signatures on a document. His reasoning is clear from the letter: "to bring us a little nearer together, I will drop my 'nom de plume,'" and he follows with his standard appeal and reasoning "only asking you <u>not</u> to make my name known to your ordinary acquaintances. The fewer strangers there are, who know my real name, the more comfortable for me: I <u>hate</u> all personal publicity."

The letter is addressed to Mrs. Jemima Rix, the mother of Edith Rix. He first wrote to Edith, whom he tutored in logic, on February 13, 1885, signing Lewis Carroll. He was replying to her solution to a published problem he presented as Lewis Carroll in *The Monthly Packet*. The clever Miss Rix and Dodgson went on to be good friends, and he dedicated his book, *A Tangled Tale*, "by Lewis Carroll" to her with an acrostic verse containing her name.

2) *"Solitude."* **By Lewis Carroll. *THE TRAIN: A FIRST-CLASS***
***MAGAZINE.* Vol. 1, March 1856, pp. 154-5.**

This is the first time the pseudonym "Lewis Carroll" was used in print.

Between March 1856 and December 1857 Carroll published eight items in *The Train*. The first, "Solitude," was an unsophisticated romantic poem treating the recapture of lost innocence and childhood. Carroll had written the story on March 16, 1853, when he was 21 years old.

The Train was a predominantly humorous magazine published monthly between 1856 and 1858 by Edmund Yates and his friends. It succeeded their defunct *Comic Times*, to which Dodgson had contributed. In response to a request from Yates for a pseudonym to attach to some verse Dodgson had submitted to the magazine, the 24 year-old Dodgson provided Yates with a list of four potential names: Edgar Cuthwellis, Edgar U. C. Westhill, Louis Carroll, and Lewis Carroll. It was Yates who chose Lewis Carroll. (See page 16 for illustration.)

3) Lewis Carroll to Dolly Draper. Autograph letter signed. May 20, 1876.

Dodgson's sense of fun, whimsy, and gamesmanship is often evidenced in his letters to young recipients and is sometimes manifested in letters in verse with acrostics. He especially liked to write verses to young ladies that incorporated a puzzle to be solved. This poem is a reply to a fan letter from Miss Dolly Draper, then 13, asking him when his birthday was. His answer, January 27, appears in the first line of the second stanza of this acrostic with her name spelled out by the first letter of each line. Dodgson had not yet met Miss Draper, so the Lewis Carroll signature on this creative work is doubly consistent with his common signature practice.

Dear Dolly, Since I do not know
Of any grander name than 'Dolly',
Let me for once address you so,
Leaving 'Miss Draper' out, although
You may be startled at my folly!

Day, 'twenty-seventh'; month, 'the first';
Rejoice that now you know the worst!
And, though you may be tall and stately,
Putting your pride a moment by,
Excuse my telling you that I
Remain yours most affectionately,
                                    Lewis Carroll.

May 20. 1876.

4) *A CHARADE.* By Lewis Carroll. April 8, 1878.

This 1878 charade (a game in which a word is represented in a riddling verse or picture) is distinguished on several counts. It is pure Lewis Carroll and signed as such, but rare in that Dodgson reproduced it (via cyclostyle*) and circulated it with a £5 offer for a similar independent charade. Moreover, it contains two lively sketches. Sketching was a constant love in Dodgson's life. He enjoyed turning out humorous designs, often adorning letters to his child-friends with them. His drawings have survived from as early as 1841, when he was nine, through the last years of his life in the 1890s. And though his drawings lack technical expertise, they are fresh, lively and, at times, outstanding artistic achievements. The ingenious answer to this charade is "I-magi-nation."

---

*Cyclostyle was a method of making ten or a dozen copies by means of a minute wheel. This was Carroll's first use of the device.

A CHARADE.

[*N.B.* FIVE POUNDS will be given to any one who succeeds in writing an original poetical Cha-rade, introducing the line "My First is followed by a bird," but making no use of the answer to this Charade. Ap. 8. 1878.
(signed)
Lewis Carroll.]

My First is singular at best:
    More plural is my Second:
My Third is far the pluralest—
So plural-plural, I protest,
    It scarcely can be reckoned!

My First is followed by a bird,
    My Second by believers
In magic art: my simple Third
Follows, too often, hopes absurd,
    And plausible deceivers.

My First to get at wisdom tries—
    A failure melancholy!
My Second men revere as wise:
My Third from heights of wisdom flies
    To depths of frantic folly!

My First is ageing day by day;
    My Second's age is ended:
My Third enjoys an age, they say,
That never seems to fade away,
    Through centuries extended!

My Whole? I need a Poet's pen
    To paint her myriad phases:
The monarch, and the slave, of men—
A mountain-summit, and a den
    Of dark and deadly mazes!

A flashing light— a fleeting shade—
    Beginning, end, and middle
Of all that human art hath made,
Or wit devised! Go, seek her aid,
    If you would guess my riddle!

5) *ALICE'S WONDERLAND BIRTHDAY BOOK.* Compiled By E. Stanley Leathes. London: Griffith and Farran, 1884.

With the fame of the *Alice* books came spin-offs, parodies, interpretations in various media, and commercial items that in the twentieth century became a veritable industry. With Dodgson's permission and obvious pleasure, *Alice's Wonderland Birthday Book* was published in 1884. It contained extracts from the *Alice* books selected by E. Stanley Leathes and blanks for each day of the year where the names of people having that birthday could be recorded. Dodgson gave the books as gifts, filling in his own name, "C. L. Dodgson," in the blank for January 27, his birthday.

But in this copy, he signs as "Lewis Carroll," and in looking-glass writing. The playful use of this reverse printing and evocation of *Alice Through the Looking-Glass* makes the use of his pen name "Lewis Carroll" consistent with his personal practice. Dodgson received his first copies of *Alice's Wonderland Birthday Book* on April 28, and this presentation copy is among the first he sent off. It is inscribed by Carroll in Dutch to Gwendolen Cecil, daughter of Lord and Lady Salisbury. Lord Salisbury was Chancellor of Oxford at the time, and Carroll was a friend of the family.

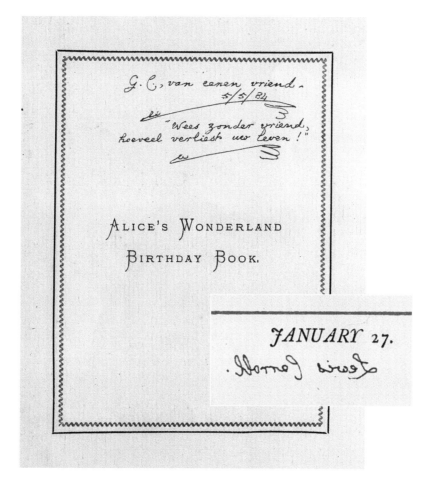

6) *THE NURSERY "ALICE."* **By Lewis Carroll.**
London: Macmillan, 1890.

Inscribed by Carroll in purple ink on the half-title: "For Elsie, from L. C. Oct. 10. 1890." Dodgson inscribed more than 100 copies of this edition. The man who used the homophonic ambiguity of "tale" and "tail" as the basis for his famous emblematic "Mouse's tale" in *Alice's Adventures in Wonderland* had a sharp ear for language and delighted in word play that extended routinely to his letter writing to his child-friends. Here Dodgson as Carroll offers a pun on the sound of his initials, "L.C.," and the pronunciation of the little girl's name.

7) Rev. C. L. Dodgson to Messrs. H. Sotheran. Autograph letter unsigned. November 15, 1890. Previously unpublished.

Christ Church, Oxford
November 15, 1890

The Rev. C. L. Dodgson is obliged to Messrs. H. Sotheran for their catalogue No. 87. He observes that at Nos. 346, 347, 348, they have inserted his name in connection with books of which he has never claimed or acknowledged the authorship, & which no one has any right to attribute to him: he will be much obliged if they will forbear from doing this for the future.

Mr. Dodgson encloses a stamped envelope in order to have the receipted bill (for 2/9) sent to him, for which he sent a postal order [D619015] for 2/6, with 3p attached in stamps on the 23 of October. He seems to have omitted to send a stamped envelope with it.

Sotheran included copies of *Alice's Adventures in Wonderland*, *The Hunting of the Snark* and *Through the Looking-Glass*, in their catalogue, attributing the books to "CARROLL (Lewis, *i.e.* Rev. C. L. Dodgson)." A clipping from the catalogue page is pasted to the letter.

Dodgson continued his dogged defense of his privacy, a campaign evident in a series of similarly written appeals and actions over the latter part of his life. His explanation for his wishing to avoid mention of his real name in conjunction with Lewis Carroll and his works was he used the name "Lewis Carroll" in order to avoid all *personal* publicity and wished to be able to go unnoticed in public places.

346 CARROLL (Lewis, *i.e.* Rev. C. L. Dodgson) ALICE'S ADVENTURES in WONDER-LAND; *with 42 illustrations by John Tenniel;* crown 8vo. *cloth, gilt edges,* 4s 6d   1877

347 CARROLL (Lewis, *i.e.* Rev. C. L. Dodgson) The HUNTING of the SNARK: an Agony, in Eight Fits; *with 9 illustrations by Henry Holiday,* FIRST EDITION, crown 8vo. *original cloth, gilt edges,* SCARCE, 9s   1876

348 CARROLL (Lewis, *i.e.* Rev. C. L. Dodgson) THROUGH the LOOKING-GLASS, and what Alice found there; FIRST EDITION, *with 50 fine engravings on wood from designs by* JOHN TENNIEL; crown 8vo. *original cloth, gilt edges,* VERY SCARCE, £1 1s   1872

8) C. L. Dodgson to Hilda Bell. Autograph letter signed. October 5, 1893.

Here in a letter to a child-friend, Dodgson writes about his pseudonym:

> And that reminds me – please tell Enid I'll write her some year. She mustn't be in such a hurry. And she mustn't get so cross about it. And I'm not exactly crushed, as yet, by her cleverness in "burying" my pseudonym of "Carroll." In fact, a more dismal failure, than she has achieved in turning it into "Carrel," I never yet met with! And I doubt very much if the girl's surname is really "Car." There is such a name: but "Carr" is much more common. And I think, if she were really a noble wise child, who can hear the sound of the tram-car rolling in the street, she'd have made a better job of burying my name!

Dodgson was at ease slipping in and out of his identities with Hilda Bell and her family because he had no need to guard his privacy. The young Hilda, her sister Enid, as well as their mother Mrs. Ethel Bell (sister of Dodgson's long-time friend Gertrude Chataway), had recently met him as Mr. Dodgson and also as Lewis Carroll. They belonged to the proper class and were the sort of eminent family Dodgson enjoyed and trusted with the knowledge of his names. While he used his books and the Lewis Carroll persona to build friendships with children, once he established a satisfactory personal relationship the open secret of his identity permitted him to move in and out of his identities with his child-friends, who were seemingly as at ease with this as he was.

9) Lewis Carroll to Edith Ball. Autograph letter signed. November 6, 1893.

Dodgson could be as playful and creative in his abundant correspondence with children as he was in the *Alice* books. His fascination with mirror reversals, so evident in the looking-glass motif in *Through the Looking-Glass*, extended to games and riddles shared in person with children and to a series of meticulously drafted looking-glass letters written backwards that required the young recipients to hold the letters up to a mirror to read them. In this fine example crafted late in Dodgson's life, one expects and finds the signature "Lewis Carroll."

10) Keepsake from Lewis Carroll's Funeral. 1898.

Lewis Carroll died at his family home at Guildford on January 14, 1898, thirteen days before his sixty-sixth birthday, from a bronchial infection perhaps exacerbated by lungs weakened from years of breathing particles from asbestos gas heaters. With his death, the secret that Charles Lutwidge Dodgson guarded from the general public–that he was the world-famous Lewis Carroll–was out. This keepsake records his dual identity, and obituaries all over the world announced that the author of *Alice's Adventures In Wonderland* and *Through the Looking-Glass* had passed away.

This keepsake is the frontispiece of the catalogue.

ALICE'S

ADVENTURES IN WONDERLAND.

BY

LEWIS CARROLL.

WITH FORTY-TWO ILLUSTRATIONS

BY

JOHN TENNIEL.

London

MACMILLAN AND CO.

1865.

[*The right of translation is reserved.*]

Item 11   Title page of the 1865 *Alice*.

II
THE 1865 *ALICE*

By Selwyn H. Goodacre

The ultimate item for any Lewis Carroll collector to possess is a copy of the fabulously rare "1865 *Alice*." So famous is this prize, that for many years it has been instantly recognizable by that name alone. A collector once told

me that when his eyes first fell on a copy in another collection, the date "1865" on the title page leapt out of the page at him. Every known copy has been individually analyzed, and every detail

London

MACMILLAN AND CO.

1865.

meticulously recorded – some even have their own nickname – "The Lost *Alice*," "The India *Alice*;" some are simply known by their location – "The British Library *Alice*," "The Huntington *Alice*."

Monographs have been devoted to single copies ("The India *Alice*" by Warren Weaver and Alfred C. Berol; Justin Schiller's 1990 volume on the "Publisher's File Copy"). There have been five complete censuses (two of them by the present writer). Copies have been lost, stolen, rebound, possibly even faked. Most have changed hands several times. Rumors about newly found copies abound.

The story of *Alice's Adventures in Wonderland* has been told many times. The tale was first narrated by Lewis Carroll on July 4, 1862, for the three daughters of Dean Liddell of Christ Church. Carroll wrote in his *Diary*:

> Duckworth and I made an expedition *up* the river to Godstow with the three Liddells: we had tea on the bank there, and did not reach Christ Church again till quarter past eight....

And later he added:

> On which occasion I told them the fairy-tale of *Alice's Adventures Underground*, which I undertook to write out for Alice....

The story, as first written, was titled *Alice's Adventures Underground*, but was then expanded to almost twice the length before it was published by the London firm of Macmillan in 1865 as *Alice's Adventures in Wonderland*.

The book was printed by the Clarendon Press, printers to Oxford University, the aim being to publish it on July 4, 1865, exactly three years after the first telling of the story on the river trip near Oxford.

Carroll had requested Macmillan to bind 50 copies for him to give away. On July 15, 1865, he noted in his *Diary*: "wrote in twenty or more copies of *Alice* to go as presents to various friends." A few days later, he heard from

John Tenniel that he was "entirely dissatisfied with the printing of the pictures," and the decision was made to withdraw the entire edition. Carroll asked recipients to return the books, promising that they would be replaced by copies of the second edition. Thirty-four copies were returned and then given away to hospitals and children's homes.

The current opinion of many is that the rejection was justified. Certainly the pictures are severely compromised by ink showing through the paper from the reverse side. For example, the White Rabbit on page one is seen against a muddy background of text from page two. In addition, the text was set up from a mixture of normal and condensed type, and the spacing between words was arbitrary and inconsistent.

We can now account for 23 copies. The Christ Church copy was first noted missing in a 1928 inventory and it was last recorded seen in 1924. Sixteen copies are now in institutional libraries (thirteen in the United States, three in the United Kingdom), and six are in private hands (four in the United States, one in the United Kingdom, and one in Switzerland).

Of the existing copies, two are from Carroll's library (one of them was returned by the actress, Marion Terry). These books were lots 680 and 681 in Carroll's estate sale catalogue. Three are presentation copies that were not returned to Carroll. Two "hospital" copies have survived. Two copies appear to be survivors from the printing shop, one being the publisher's file copy. Six survivors have either parts or whole pages from the books' preliminary leaves missing, and so may be hospital, or presentation copies with presentation inscriptions removed, either at the time, or by later owners. One could even be the lost Christ Church copy. There are ten copies whose earliest provenance is unknown.

Any copy of the 1865 *Alice* is highly desirable (and highly valuable), but copies in the original red cloth binding must be the most coveted.

Jon Lindseth acquired the William Self copy in 1997. It is one of the ten existing copies in the original red cloth, and if the condition of the binding is the criterion, it would appear to be ranked second or third in order of quality. This copy was probably owned originally by George William Kitchin, a colleague of Lewis Carroll's at Christ Church, and Secretary of the School Book Committee for the University Press. He later gave the book to his daughter, Alexandra "Xie" Rhoda Kitchin (b. 1864), who was to become one of Carroll's favorite child-friends. She sold the book at auction in 1925, but, sadly, died on the day of the sale. Dr. A. S.W. Rosenbach acquired it for the Pforzheimer Library, and as part of that collection, it was one of nine 1865 *Alice's* featured in the Columbia University Centenary Exhibition in 1932. The Pforzheimer Library sold their copy to Harriet Borland in 1974. In 1976, her library was sold, and the book was acquired by the Los Angeles film producer, William Self, who sold it to Jon Lindseth.

With this copy, we have a wonderful opportunity to see an example of the book in its proper original state, with the text and binding as they were when the book was first produced. Warren Weaver pointed out in 1971 that there are two variant states of the book. This is because the second preliminary gathering [b^2] was printed in duplicate, and the two settings differ in several respects. (One leaf has the end of the prefatory poem, the second is the "Contents" page.)

In Variant A, the first line of the last stanza of the prefatory poem reads "Alice! A..."; in the list of Contents, RABBIT HOLE does not have a hyphen, the "9" in page numbers 29 and 59 is round, is oval in page 95, and the 5 in page 95 is broken in the foot.

Alice ! A childish story take,

And with a gentle hand

Lay it where Childhood's dreams are twined

In Memory's mystic band,

Like pilgrim's withered wreath of flowers

CONTENTS.

CHAPTER		PAGE
I.	DOWN THE RABBIT HOLE	1
II.	THE POOL OF TEARS......................	15
III.	A CAUCUS-RACE AND A LONG TALE	29
IV.	THE RABBIT SENDS IN A LITTLE BILL..........	41
V.	ADVICE FROM A CATERPILLAR	59
VI.	PIG AND PEPPER	76
VII.	A MAD TEA-PARTY	95
VIII.	THE QUEEN'S CROQUET-GROUND	112
IX.	THE MOCK TURTLE'S STORY	130
X.	THE LOBSTER QUADRILLE...	147

Variant A of the 1865 *Alice.*

In Variant a, the first line of the last stanza of the prefatory poem reads "Alice! a..."; in the list of Contents, RABBIT-HOLE has a hyphen, the "9" in page numbers 29 and 59 is oval, is round in 95, and the 5 in page 95 is undamaged.

The Lindseth copy is an example of Variant a. Illustrations that accompany this essay show the differences in the two variants. They are shown here in print for the first time.

> Alice ! a childish story take,
>   And with a gentle hand
> Lay it where Childhood's dreams are twined
>   In Memory's mystic band,
> Like pilgrim's withered wreath of flowers

CONTENTS.

CHAPTER		PAGE
I.	DOWN THE RABBIT-HOLE	1
II.	THE POOL OF TEARS	15
III.	A CAUCUS-RACE AND A LONG TALE	29
IV.	THE RABBIT SENDS IN A LITTLE BILL	41
V.	ADVICE FROM A CATERPILLAR	59
VI.	PIG AND PEPPER	76
VII.	A MAD TEA-PARTY	95
VIII.	THE QUEEN'S CROQUET-GROUND	112
IX.	THE MOCK TURTLE'S STORY	130

Variant a of the 1865 *Alice*.

ITEM EXHIBITED

11) ***ALICE'S ADVENTURES IN WONDERLAND.* By Lewis Carroll. London: Macmillan, 1865.**

This is one of 23 known copies of the 1865 *Alice.* It is in original red cloth and is the "Alice! a" version. The second preliminary gathering [b^2] was printed in duplicate and the two differ as shown in the illustrations on pages 31 and 32.

King.	Richard 3.rd
Queen.	Queen Eleanor.
Hero.	Buffalo Bill.
Poet.	The writer of the "Bab" ballads.
Artist.	Vermicelli di Napoli.
Author.	Johnsonius Dictionaries.
Virtue.	That which meets with more than its own reward.
Colour.	Crushed-strawberry.
Air.	"Knock'd 'em in the Old Kent Road"!
Dish.	Sheep's head. & Trotters.
Flower.	Cauli-flower.
Costume.	Pyjamas.
Name.	Jemima-ann.
Occupation.	Building Castles (en Espagne)
Amusement.	Riding my Gee-gee—& other "Hobbies"!
Motto.	"Better late than never."
Dislike	Being "Interviewed"!!!
Locality.	My own "den"!
Ambition.	Gave it up long ago.!!!

John Tenniel.

[J] Augt. 16. 1893.

Item 18   Tenniel's list of "Favorite Things."

III

Sir John Tenniel and Lewis Carroll

By Rodney Engen

Throughout the 1860s John Tenniel was in great demand as a black and white illustrator for magazines and books. His greatest challenge – the *Alice* commissions – would appear during that period and their genesis highlights the role and the plight of the so-called "Sixties School" illustrator, his engravers and publishers.

The now well-documented *Alice* story began on a boat trip with Lewis Carroll and the Liddell sisters in Oxford in July 1862. At that time Carroll was pressed to entertain the young objects of his affection with a story. Gradually, over the year, he embellished his tale of Alice and wrote chapter headings for it, spinning out what he called that "interminable fairy-tale." He wrote up the tale and proposed to give his own illustrated edition to young Alice Liddell for Christmas that year. But the project took off and he did not finish until February of the following year. He had added his own illustrations, 37 in number, and by July had decided to publish it.

Carroll was a keen but deficient amateur artist who had enthusiasm but lacked technical skill. He especially found animal drawings difficult. He much admired Tenniel's *Aesop* and *Punch* animal fillers and he decided to write to the *Punch* journalist Tom Taylor for an introduction to Tenniel. Carroll visited Tenniel's studio in January 1864, and by April 5 he had his agreement to illustrate *Alice*. But Tenniel was inundated with work at the time and his agreement meant little to the book's production schedule. Moreover, while Carroll waited for Tenniel, he decided to expand the manuscript to almost twice its original size.

Tenniel delayed work for a further two months, during which time his beloved mother died, followed by the death of his friend and *Punch* mentor, John Leech. Both deaths seriously affected his work and undermined his ambition. Finally, over a six-month period, Tenniel produced the necessary 42 drawings to be wood engraved by the Dalziels, completing the last one on April 18, 1865.

From the start, the collaboration between Carroll and Tenniel was a turbulent one. They had similar personalities, both being fastidious and preoccupied, if not obsessed, by their work. Carroll felt, as the commissioning agent, he could provide Tenniel with models and suggestions for his illustrations – he had after all originally illustrated the story himself. These Tenniel accepted but ignored. It soon became clear that Tenniel was expected to be a mere technician, complacent, without a will of his own, someone hired to polish and perfect Carroll's original ideas.

Carroll had admired Tenniel's whimsy in *Punch*, and here were the gnomish fantasies which helped Carroll with his original drawings for *Alice*.

Such was Carroll's fastidiousness and concern that he sent Tenniel a detailed list of the drawings required, with dimensions and placement upon the page in a mathematical code. Tenniel found such demands tiresome and upsetting. He felt they undermined his creativity.

It is true to say that most of the book's invention came from Carroll. His original sketches indicate how he wanted Alice portrayed in her various settings and guises. The idea of claustrophobia, in which Alice fills a small space, was merely polished and given context as he borrowed a favorite device of Rossetti's with a darkened room, opened diamond-paned window, with Alice's arm reaching out to emphasize her trapped state.

For all his illustrations, Tenniel adopted his *Punch* technique by making preliminary sketches of each design in pencil, later in pen and ink with Chinese white to simulate engraved lines. He used tracing paper to transfer the bare pencil outline of each composition onto the woodblock and finished off the shading on the block with one of his favorite hard 6H pencils, the block first being whitened to help direct the engravers.

Item 12

Tenniel worked closely with the engravers, the Dalziel Brothers [Item 12]. He received proofs of sections of his drawings, a face or a figure without the background, which he corrected and sent back. His perfectionist instincts were encouraged by the process.

Sometimes Carroll objected to Tenniel's inventions and the apparent liberties he took. Alice's balloon-like crinoline, for example, was found objectionable and Tenniel offered to change this to draped ruffles in the final engraved version of *Through the Looking-Glass*.

Similarly the Hatta in prison was altered several times, even after it had been engraved, the engraver having to cut out each offending section of the block and "plug" it in the new version, as proofs in the Victoria and Albert Museum suggest.

Moreover, Tenniel sought out his own models. A sketchbook, (now in the Huntington Library), has a pencil drawn thistle which provides botanical evidence for another *Alice* illustration. Much had been made of Tenniel's (or Carroll's for that matter) models, and conjecture included such sources as paintings in the National Gallery (for the Ugly Duchess) and medieval manuscripts. Carroll, too, had his own ideas: he declared the Queen of Hearts must be made into the "embodiment of ungovernable passion"– which must have proved a trial for Tenniel.

Alice finally appeared at the end of June 1865, when 2,000 copies were printed. The total cost was revealing: it nearly amounted to Tenniel's annual *Punch* salary of £500: Tenniel was paid £138 for his drawings, the engravers, the Dalziel Brothers, £142, the printers, the Clarendon Press, were paid £137, and binding and advertising cost £80. This was a considerable amount of money for such a speculative venture and it is understandable why Carroll was so upset when Tenniel rejected the printing and insisted the book was too poorly done to be made public. He insisted that at least nine of his illustrations were too dark, and that nine were too light.

Eventually Carroll agreed and the first edition was suppressed and a new edition ordered from a different printer. It remains a fascinating puzzle just how badly printed the first edition really was. Some have suggested Tenniel was merely trying to get back at Carroll for being so mistreated. Comparisons between proofs and the first edition and the new published edition reveal little seriously wrong. The Dalziel proofs in the British Museum make fascinating objects of reference in this regard.

In the end, Carroll recovered part of his losses by selling the first edition sheets to D. Appleton and Co., an American publisher. A satisfactory new edition was issued in 1866 and in just two years Carroll made a healthy profit of £250 on his *Alice*. Since all books were printed from electrotype rather than the original woodblocks, the blocks remained in excellent condition [Item 17].

The success of the *Alice* book followed Tenniel and, although generally self-effacing about his work, he was proud of his reception. He was persuaded by his *Punch* colleagues to parody it in various ways for his weekly political cartoon and would later make copies of his favorite illustrations when asked to do so [Item 14].

So heartened was Carroll by the success of his *Alice* that within months of its publication he proposed a sequel which he then called *Looking-glass House*. Knowing illustrations were the key to its success, he again asked Tenniel to help him, but Tenniel flatly refused. He pleaded the pressures of work and Carroll was forced to try other artists, but he found no one willing or suitable, having discounted the well-known illustrator, Richard Doyle, and, having been refused by Noel Paton, who claimed, "Tenniel's the man."

Eventually Tenniel agreed and it would take a further three years before his illustrations finally appeared in *Through the Looking-Glass*. Again the venture was plagued by delays and intransigence on Tenniel's part. Tenniel objected to certain passages like the now famous "A Wasp in a Wig" chapter which he refused to draw, "because it does not interest me in the least, and I can't see my way to picture it." His Jabberwocky was thought too terrifying for the frontispiece and was pushed further into the book. Again models were a source of debate and mystery: some believed Tenniel to be the White Knight, the Lion and Unicorn were Gladstone and Disraeli, and Humpty Dumpty was thought to be Mark Lemon, a founding editor of *Punch*.

Through the Looking-Glass was finally printed in November 1871. The book had left Tenniel completely shattered and disillusioned about illustrating on wood again. "I am completely weary of drawing on wood, perfectly sick of wood engraving," he wrote to the *Once a Week* publisher. The book and his relationship with Carroll had left a serious mark upon his career. With a hint of relief in his tone he wrote about this years later: " It is a curious fact that with *Through the Looking-Glass* the faculty of making drawings for book illustrations parted from me, and notwithstanding all sorts of tempting inducements, I have done nothing in that direction since."

Instead Tenniel returned happily to *Punch* and worked there for another 20 years. A key figure in Victorian England, he was a supreme Victorian with a voluminous number of admirers. He was knighted for his efforts, a fact which greatly embarrassed him. He was to the end a self-effacing, dry-witted character [Item 18]. But it was his *Alice* books which remain his greatest monument today. As Austin Dobson wrote so prophetically:

> *Enchanting ALICE! Black-and-white*
> *Has made your deeds perennial;*
> *And naught save "Chaos and old Night"*
> *Can part you now from TENNIEL.*

The items exhibited in this section show many aspects of the *Alice* collaborations by John Tenniel and Lewis Carroll. A thorough investigation of their relationship will be found in my biography of Tenniel, *Alice's White Knight*, Scolar Press, 1991.

ITEMS EXHIBITED

12) John Tenniel to Dalziel. Autograph letter signed.

10 Portsdown Road.
Wednesday.

Dear Dalziel.

　　Be so good as to send a <u>complete</u> proof next time as I want to send it to Mr. Dodgson.
　　I have two more drawings ready for you.
　　Yours very truly
　　　　(Signed with Tenniel's monogram)

The Dalziel Brothers were the wood engravers for both *Alice's Adventures in Wonderland* and *Through the Looking-Glass*. (See page 36 for illustration.)

13) *ALICE'S ADVENTURES IN WONDERLAND.* **By Lewis Carroll. London: Macmillan, 1868. Eleventh thousand.**

Signed in black ink on the half-title, "CLD," in Carroll's familiar interlaced initials. Also in Carroll's autograph on the recto of the lower free end paper "P. 132. last line – for *very many* read *every body*." The correction first appeared in the fourteenth thousand of 1869. Also in Tenniel's autograph in black ink on the half-title: "John Tenniel. 1898." The signature and date were likely done with different pens. One can only speculate if this book was purchased by Tenniel at the Carroll estate sale or signed by Tenniel for the purchaser. This book was lot 684 in the estate sale catalogue.

14) *THROUGH THE LOOKING-GLASS.* By Lewis Carroll. London: Macmillan, 1872.

With two Tenniel pencil drawings bound in. Both are signed with his monogram and are on heavy drawing paper. It was common for artists of the time to earn extra income by redrawing their popular illustrations and Tenniel was no exception.

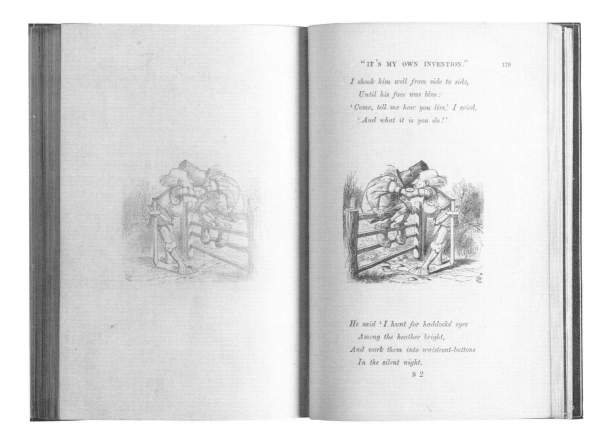

15) *THROUGH THE LOOKING-GLASS.* **By Lewis Carroll.**
London: Macmillan, 1872.

Inscribed by Tenniel in black ink on the half-title: "To Mrs Fred Evans. With [Tenniel's monogram]'s kindest regards Christmas 1871." And with Tenniel's pencil drawing, "Alice with the golden crown," signed with his monogram. Tenniel must have felt very good about this book at the time of publication as he inscribed a number of copies, often adding an extra pencil illustration.

16) *ALICE'S ADVENTURES UNDER GROUND.* By Lewis Carroll. London: Macmillan, 1886.

Inscribed by Lewis Carroll in purple ink on the half-title: "John Tenniel from the Author Jan. 1887." Carroll continued to send Tenniel inscribed copies of his books long after Tenniel illustrated the *Alice* books. So their relationship, at least from Carroll's view, must have been satisfactory.

17) Original electrotype of the frontispiece for *Alice's Adventures in Wonderland,* People's Edition (1887).

Carroll insisted that the illustrations for his books be printed using electrotypes in order to preserve the fragile and expensive boxwood blocks. To make an "electro," as they are called, the original relief engraved wood block was pressed into a block of warm beeswax. This wax mold was then covered with powdered graphite and by electroysis a copper layer was deposited on it. The wax was melted out and the copper surface backed up with another metal to make an exact duplicate of the boxwood block's engraved surface.

18) Tenniel's list of "Favorite Things." Autograph manuscript signed. August 16, 1893.

This was evidently a Victorian parlor game as other autograph versions have been seen. Tenniel's sense of humor and wit come through clearly here. (See page 34 for illustration.)

19) *BLEAK HOUSE*. By Charles Dickens. London: Bradbury and Evans, 1853.

Inscribed in blue ink on the dedication page: "John Tenniel from Charles Dickens Third October 1853." Dickens had invited the 33 year-old Tenniel to play the part of Hodge in his amateur acting company's performance of Bulwer Lytton's "Not So Bad As We Seem." Far from a typical amateur company, the play received a royal premiere before Queen Victoria.

PROCEEDINGS OF

THE ROYAL SOCIETY.

VOL. XV. No. 84.

CONTENTS.

PAGE

On the Mysteries of Numbers alluded to by Fermat. By the Rt. Hon.
Sir FREDERICK POLLOCK, Lord Chief Baron, F.R.S., &c. 115

May 3, 1866.

I. Report on the Levelling from the Mediterranean to the Dead Sea. By
Colonel Sir HENRY JAMES, R.E., F.R.S. 128

II. Note on the Amyl-Compounds derived from Petroleum. By C. SCHOR-
LEMMER 131

III. On a New Series of Hydrocarbons derived from Coal-tar. By C. SCHOR-
LEMMER 132

IV. The Calculus of Chemical Operations; being a Method for the Investigation,
by means of Symbols, of the Laws of the Distribution of Weight in
Chemical Change. Part I.—On the Construction of Chemical Symbols.
By Sir B. C. BRODIE, Bart., F.R.S., Professor of Chemistry in the University of Oxford 136

May 17, 1866.

I. On the Motion of a Rigid Body moving freely about a Fixed Point. By
J. J. SYLVESTER, LL.D., F.R.S. 139

II. On Appold's Apparatus for regulating Temperature and keeping the Air in
a Building at any desired degree of Moisture. By J. P. GASSIOT, Esq.,
V.P.R.S. 144

III. On the Spectrum of a New Star in Corona Borealis. By WILLIAM
HUGGINS, F.R.S., and W. A. MILLER, M.D., V.-P. and Treas. R.S. . 146

IV. Condensation of Determinants, being a new and brief Method for computing
their arithmetical values. By the Rev. C. L. DODGSON, M.A., Student of
Christ Church, Oxford 150

May 31, 1866.

I. An Account of Experiments in some of which Electroscopic Indications of
Animal Electricity were detected for the first time by a new method of
experimenting. By CHARLES BLAND RADCLIFFE, M.D., Fellow of the
Royal College of Physicians in London, Physician to the Westminster
Hospital and to the National Hospital for Paralysis and Epilepsy, &c. . 156

II. On the Dynamical Theory of Gases. By J. CLERK MAXWELL, F.R.S. L. & E. 167

III. On the means of increasing the Quantity of Electricity given by Induction-
Machines. By the Rev. T. ROMNEY ROBINSON, D.D., F.R.S. . . . 171

IV. On the Stability of Domes. By E. WYNDHAM TARN, M.A. 182

[The continuation of this Paper will be given in the next Number.]

TAYLOR AND FRANCIS, RED LION COURT, FLEET STREET.

Item 24   Includes Dodgson's paper, "Condensation of Determinants."

IV
Charles L. Dodgson, Mathematician

By Francine F. Abeles

Charles L. Dodgson's publications on mathematics and on subjects intimately related to mathematics offer a very different picture of the man made famous by his *Alice* books. The reserved bachelor, known for his whimsy and nonsense writing, was quite an activist – involved in issues of local governance at Oxford University, in problems of national politics at the highest level, and in educational reform affecting the very core of the British system. His purely mathematical pursuits incorporated inexorable logical arguments that produced notable new results of which several were developed further by mathematicians in this century. The items displayed in this exhibition allow the viewer to sample some of Dodgson's most significant work. Other items in the Lindseth Collection provide further evidence that deepens the substance of this less well-known side of the man better known as Lewis Carroll.

As a member of the Governing Body of Christ Church, Dodgson became involved in local issues like designs for buildings and awarding fellowships, and in the University, in such matters as conditions of employment of professors. Later in his life he became absorbed with the questions of political representation and franchise affecting the entire country. He recorded aspects of these involvements in his *Diaries*, in private letters to political figures, in public letters to newspapers, in the publication of humorous pamphlets, and, more significantly, in pamphlets addressing the bases of the controversies. Dodgson applied principles of logical reasoning and simple mathematical techniques to create novel solutions to the elements that all political processes ultimately share – voting and elections.

Issues of fairness, as in minority representation, particularly intrigued him. The early set of three pamphlets, two of which are in this exhibition [Items 20 & 21], reflect the changes in his thinking about how a committee should select the best candidate or proposal. On the strength of these completely original pamphlets, Dodgson is considered as a voting theorist, second only to the great eighteenth-century figure, the Marquis de Condorcet.

Originating from these are the four items on tennis tournaments which first appeared in the *St. James's Gazette*. In the pamphlet included in this exhibition [Item 22], Dodgson initiated the mathematical subject of the best possible procedures to choose the top candidates, applying it to the problem of properly selecting the first three winners. In the Introduction, Dodgson addresses the underlying issue of fairness, that of a player who had been eliminated early on and has seen the second prize given to another player whom he knew to be inferior to himself.

The Principles of Parliamentary Representation [Item 23], was followed by a *Supplement* and a *Postscript to Supplement* (both in the Lindseth Collection). In addition to letters on the topic appearing in the *St. James's Gazette*, Dodgson sent copies of letters and his pamphlets to William Gladstone, to Lord Salisbury, with whom he was friendly, and to other political leaders. Dodgson first wrote about proportional representation in connection with a proposal by the Governing Body of Christ Church to elect members to the "Electoral Board" so that a minority of voters could elect one member. This pamphlet is the first written work in which both apportionment – assigning seats to multimember districts, and proportional representation – assigning seats to political parties within districts – are treated formally together.

The theory of determinants was developed in the nineteenth century in Britain, and Dodgson's book, *An Elementary Treatise on Determinants*...[Item 25], was among the first published on the subject. Correspondence between March 1866 and November 1867 establishes not only Dodgson's profound understanding of this theory, but also that his work was known and well-regarded by other members of the British mathematical community, especially William Spottiswoode, author of the first textbook on the subject, and later, President of the London Mathematical Society and of the Royal Society. We know that Dodgson first began to work on the book from his *Diary* entry of October 28, 1865, so the condensation process [Item 24], is one of the outcomes of the research for his textbook. A version of it appears as Appendix II of the book.

As a college teacher of mathematics, Dodgson was concerned about helping students learn to reason logically. Geometry was the vehicle, but his concern was much broader. To Dodgson, logical reasoning could establish truths, and knowing the truth was an essential element for making the right decisions in everyday life.

Euclid's geometry was embedded in the English educational system, and performing well on examinations was a key to future success. As Dodgson saw it, having a large number of different textbooks would wreak havoc in the administration of the examinations. A particular concern, alternatives for Euclid's parallel postulate, offered by the "rivals" in *Euclid and His Modern Rivals, (EMR)*, and in the *Supplement* [Items 26 a, b and 27], he found wanting. An offprint of Appendix IV of *EMR*, *The various methods of treating Parallels, adopted by Euclid and his Modern Rivals* is also in the Lindseth Collection.

Favorable reviews of Dodgson's theoretical book on geometry, *Curiosa Mathematica. Part I...* [Item 28], in popular journals like the *Academy*, *Athenaeum*, *Cambridge Review*, and *Nature*, exhibit a lack of understanding of Dodgson's ideas. For example, the *Academy* reviewer wrote on February 9, 1889, that Dodgson did not connect his work with the development of non-Euclidean geometry. But Dodgson was not interested in which geometry models physical space. He wanted to find a better Euclidean parallel axiom, one that would not appeal to infinity and infinitesimals, uncharted territory at that time. And contrary to the reviewer's comment, Dodgson did address the failure of his axiom in a non-Euclidean setting – on pp. xvi-xvii of the first edition of the book.

The ability to do rapid mental calculations was very important to Dodgson and he devised many methods to help others acquire the skill. Like logical reasoning, he considered it essential for the demands of daily life. One of these methods, finding the day of the week if the date is known, is the content of item 29a. This, together with the difficult calculation of the date of Easter Sunday, are the ingredients of a perpetual calendar. In his (unpublished) *Diary* entry of May 7, 1897, Dodgson comments on the Easter Rule, devised originally by the great mathematician, Carl Friedrich Gauss (who died in 1855), and reported by W.W.R. Ball in his book, *Mathematical Recreations and Problems*. In an unpublished manuscript, Dodgson simplified it so that the date could be calculated mentally.

Dodgson resigned his teaching post in 1881 to leave more time for other interests. As the items in this exhibition attest, he remained mathematically creative into the final decade of his life.

ITEMS EXHIBITED

20) *SUGGESTIONS AS TO THE BEST METHOD OF TAKING VOTES, WHERE MORE THAN TWO ISSUES ARE TO BE VOTED ON*. Oxford: E. Pickard Hall and J.H. Stacy, 1874.

In the 1870s, Dodgson wrote three pamphlets applying his mathematical skills to the political procedures operating in the committees that are ubiquitous in academic life. In this item he proposes that when a first ballot does not produce an absolute majority for a candidate, all candidates should then be compared in pairs. His method was used by the Governing Body of Christ Church to choose the architect from the group of four finalists who had submitted designs for the new belfry of Christ Church.

SUGGESTIONS

AS TO THE BEST METHOD OF

TAKING VOTES,

WHERE MORE THAN

TWO ISSUES ARE TO BE VOTED ON.

OXFORD:
BY E. PICKARD HALL AND J. H. STACY,
Printers to the University.
1874.

21) *A METHOD OF TAKING VOTES ON MORE THAN TWO ISSUES.* March 1876.

This pamphlet, the last in the set of three on the theory of committees, and the most important, appears here in two versions: one containing numerous corrections by Dodgson; the other an amended version. The setting for this work was Dodgson's disagreement with the conditions of a plan to retain a distinguished Oxford professor that was passed on February 15th. Dodgson proposes a method of ranking candidates in an election in the presence of "cyclical majorities," when no candidate can achieve a simple majority over each of the others. This method, which produces a unique ranking of all the candidates, anticipates a probability model first described formally in 1964.

22) *LAWN TENNIS TOURNAMENTS. THE TRUE METHOD OF ASSIGNING PRIZES WITH A PROOF OF THE FALLACY OF THE PRESENT METHOD.* By Charles L. Dodgson, M.A. London: Macmillan, 1883.

Lawn Tennis is a variant of the game introduced in 1874 in England. Dodgson considered the method used to select the second and third best players in tennis competitions faulty and, consequently, unfair. This pamphlet is an extension of the work he did earlier [Item 21] to choose the winner from a ranked set of candidates in the presence of "cyclical majorities." Although his tournament is not optimal, making more comparisons than needed, it is the seed of the modern idea of a "covering relation," which has been used since 1980 to identify the best set of proposals when majority preferences are represented as tournament graphs.

23) *THE PRINCIPLES OF PARLIAMENTARY REPRESENTATION.*
By Charles L. Dodgson, M.A. London: Harrison and Sons, 1884.

Dodgson wrote this pamphlet to influence the outcome of two proposed electoral reforms (passed in 1884-85): an extension of the franchise and a re-distribution of seats in the House of Commons. As Dodgson saw it, using the proposed plurality voting rule in single-member districts, with roughly an equal number of supporters, could result in a disproportionate number of seats being allotted to the larger Liberal party at the expense of the smaller Conservative party. The pamphlet has the form of a long, rigorously logical argument with few of the trappings of formal mathematics. Its basis is the "zero-sum game," a concept not fully developed until 1928.

24) *"Condensation of Determinants, Being A New And Brief Method For Computing Their Arithmetical Values."* By the Rev. C. L. Dodgson, M.A. *PROCEEDINGS OF THE ROYAL SOCIETY.* Vol. XV, No. 84, 1866, pp. 150-55.

Dodgson's best known work in linear algebra is this remarkable labor-saving algorithm. Read by Bartholomew Price to The Royal Society on May 17, 1866, condensation is a method for computing the determinant of a higher order matrix that avoids the extensive calculations required by the standard method of his time. Condensation has appeared in several texts on numerical analysis in this century, and was used in an early step toward the solution in the 1980s of an important open problem in combinatorics known as the Macdonald Conjecture. (See page 44 for illustration.)

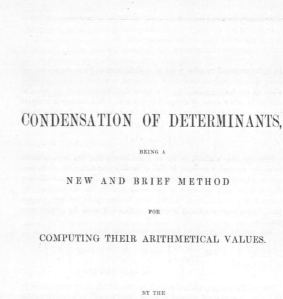

[*From the* PROCEEDINGS OF THE ROYAL SOCIETY, No. 84, 1866.]

CONDENSATION OF DETERMINANTS,

BEING A

NEW AND BRIEF METHOD

FOR

COMPUTING THEIR ARITHMETICAL VALUES.

BY THE

REV. C. L. DODGSON, M.A.,
STUDENT OF CHRIST CHURCH, OXFORD.

Offprint from the *Proceedings Of The Royal Society.*

25) *AN ELEMENTARY TREATISE ON DETERMINANTS WITH THEIR APPLICATION TO SIMULTANEOUS LINEAR EQUATIONS AND ALGEBRAICAL GEOMETRY.* **By Charles L. Dodgson, M.A. London: Macmillan, 1867.**

Inscribed to his friend and mathematical mentor at Oxford, Professor Bartholomew Price, the book is Dodgson's most significant work on this subject. *Determinants* provides a tool to state results about the solutions of systems of equations. Perhaps his emphasis on exact logical reasoning, odd notation and unusual terminology is the reason it has taken more than a century to recognize that the book contains the first written proof of a standard theorem connecting the rank of a matrix with the existence of solutions to certain linear systems. (See Chapter IV, Proposition II.)

AN

ELEMENTARY TREATISE

ON

DETERMINANTS

WITH THEIR APPLICATION TO

SIMULTANEOUS LINEAR EQUATIONS
AND ALGEBRAICAL GEOMETRY.

BY

CHARLES L. DODGSON, M.A.

STUDENT AND MATHEMATICAL LECTURER OF CHRIST CHURCH, OXFORD.

26) a. *EUCLID AND HIS MODERN RIVALS.* **By Charles L. Dodgson, M.A. London: Macmillan, 1879. First Edition.**

Dodgson's best known work on geometry, this book, written in the form of a drama in four acts using dialogue that is both satirical and witty, is his answer to the swarm of books written in the period 1860–1879 that were being considered as replacements for Euclid's *Elements* in the teaching of elementary geometry. Dismissing them one by one, Dodgson shows that Euclid's text should be retained.

b. *EUCLID AND HIS MODERN RIVALS.* **By Charles L. Dodgson, M.A. London: Macmillan, 1885. Second Edition.**

In the second edition, Dodgson substantially simplifies his notation, resulting in the elimination of two of the original six appendices, (III and IV) and adds a fourteenth rival, Olaus Henrici's geometry text, as Act II, Scene V. The reworked frontispiece now includes all the theorems of Book I of Euclid.

27) *SUPPLEMENT TO "EUCLID AND HIS MODERN RIVALS" CONTAINING A NOTICE OF HENRICI'S GEOMETRY TOGETHER WITH SELECTIONS FROM THE REVIEWS.* By C. L. Dodgson. London: Macmillan, 1885.

Inscribed by Dodgson: "R.E.B. from C.L.D. Nov. 27, 1890." This is possibly R. E. Baynes, a Christ Church colleague.

Paginated continuously with the first edition of *Euclid And His Modern Rivals*, Henrici's book here is Act II, Scene VI. Appendix VII contains reviews of *EMR* with Dodgson's remarks interspersed. Long reviews appeared in such popular journals as the *English Mechanic*, the *Saturday Review, Nature, The Examiner,* and the *Educational Times.*

In the *Saturday Review,* we see for the first time that Dodgson was aware of the existence of other geometries in which the Euclidean parallel axiom is denied (pp. 338-9).

Through a given point outside a straig... can be drawn to it. This at once raises the question, What business have you to assume that *any* parallel can be drawn? in other words, that parallels can and do exist in plane geometry, and that there is no external point through which a parallel cannot be drawn? The assumption, be it observed, is not made by Euclid. And we may further observe that it is not such a small one as it looks, especially in the light of modern geometrical speculations. [*But who in the world* wants *to make this assumption?*] For it results from the work of Lobatschewsky and others that our actual geometry is not an elucidation of eternal and immutable and unique relations, but is rather in the nature of a purely physical science. That is to say, it is the investigation of properties of space, or of things in so far as they occupy space, which might quite conceivably have been different. A consistent geometry (though of course inapplicable to our real experience) can be, and has been, founded on the categorical denial of Playfair's axiom. Euclid's geometry is the science, not of space absolutely, but of a particular kind

Page 338 from the *Saturday Review.* The comment in square brackets is Dodgson's.

28) *CURIOSA MATHEMATICA. PART I. A NEW THEORY OF PARALLELS*. **By Charles L. Dodgson, M.A. London: Macmillan, 1888, first edition and third edition, 1890.**

Less well-known than *Euclid And His Modern Rivals*, this book is arguably the most significant of Dodgson's books on geometry. The frontispiece is his clever alternative to Euclid's parallel postulate, Axiom 6: in every circle the inscribed equilateral hexagon is greater [in area] than any one of the segments lying outside it. Beginning with the third edition, this is Axiom I of Book II, and a tetragon is substituted for the hexagon. In Appendix II, he develops a theory of infinitesimals that, although flawed, contains elements that were important in the rigorous theory created in the 1960s.

29) a. *"To Find The Day Of The Week For Any Given Date."* By Lewis Carroll. *NATURE* Vol. XXXV, March 31, 1887, p. 517.

Dodgson published three articles in *Nature*. In this article he gives a method for finding the day of the week, if the date is known, that he believed could be calculated mentally in 15 to 25 seconds. Dodgson wrote in his *Diary* that he discovered the rule on March 8, 1887.

b. C. L. Dodgson to Mr. Thoms [*sic*]. Autograph letter signed. September 8, 1897. Previously unpublished. (Most likely to David Thomas, a fellow of Trinity College.)

2. Bedford Well Road,
Eastbourne. Sep. 8/97

Dear Mr. Thoms,

Please excuse brevity: I'm awfully busy. Zeller's Formula is quoted by Mr. W. W. Rouse Ball, in his "Mathematical Recreations," p. 242 of the 4th edition. (It is published by Macmillan & Co.) He seems to have found it in Zeller's "Acta Mathematica," Stockholm, 1887, vol IX, pp. 131 to 136. He states it thus – Let $\{N/x\}$ mean "integral part of quotient when N is divided by x" – And let the pth day of the qth month of the year N be the rth day of the week. Then r is the remainder when $(p+2q + \{3(q+1)/5\}+N+\{N/4\}-7)$ is divided by 7, provided Jan. & Feb. are taken as 13th and 14th months of preceding year. The value of η is, for O.S., "O"; for N.S., "$\{N/100\}-\{N/400\}-2$."

Can you find day of week, for any date, in your head? And in what time? I have devised a rule by which I can find it, in my head, in about 25 seconds. Also I have condensed Gauss' Rule for finding Easter Day for any year, & can find it, in my head, in about 40 seconds.

Very truly yours, C.L. Dodgson.

2. Bedford Well Road,
Eastbourne. Sep. 8/97

Dear Mr. Thoms,

Please excuse brevity: I'm awfully busy. Zeller's Formula is quoted by Mr. W.W. Rouse Ball, in his "Mathematical Recreations", p. 242 of the 4th edition. (It is published by Macmillan & Co.) He seems to have found it in Zeller's "Acta Mathematica", Stockholm, 1887, vol IX., pp. 131 to 136. He states it thus – Let $\{N/x\}$ mean "integral part of quotient when N is divided by x." And let the pth day of the qth month of the year N be the rth day of the week.

Then r is the remainder when $(p + 2q + \{3(q+1)/5\} + N + \{N/4\} - \eta)$ is divided by 7, provided Jan. & Feb. are taken as 13th & 14th months of preceding year. The value of η is, for O.S., "0"; for N.S., "$\{N/100\} - \{N/400\} - 2$."

Can you find day of week, for any date, in your head? And in what time? I have devised a rule by which I can find it, in my head, in about 25 seconds. Also I have condensed Gauss' Rule for finding Easter Day for any year, & can find it, in my head, in about 40 seconds.

Very truly yours, C.L. Dodgson.

Ten years after his article in *Nature*, Dodgson submitted one of his eleven problem-questions to the *Educational Times* (published September 1, 1897) eliciting information about a completely arithmetic method given by Christopher Zeller. This letter is the only evidence that Dodgson had read Zeller's formula in the book by Rouse Ball – but in the third edition (1896), not the fourth which was published in 1905 and is mistakenly referred to in the letter.

In the garden of Elm Lodge. Hampstead

Mrs. George MacDonald. Grevilla. Mary. C.L. Dodgson. Irene. Grace

Item 35   Lewis Carroll and the MacDonald family, July 1863.

V

Lewis Carroll's Photography

By Edward Wakeling

On the last day of 1856, Lewis Carroll wrote in his *Diary*: "I hope to make good progress in Photography…it is my one recreation, and I think should be done well." Earlier in the year, inspired by his maternal uncle, R. W. Skeffington Lutwidge, and instructed by his colleague and friend, Reginald Southey, he began his photographic hobby and it occupied much of his spare time for the next 24 years. Carroll had ordered a folding camera from the London camera maker, Ottewill, on March 18, 1856, and it arrived on May 1. He began taking photographs with it that same day, and a week later, with Southey's help, he took his first self-portrait.

From the outset, Carroll was methodical about his photography, numbering his glass-plate negatives and the prints made from each plate, and keeping a list of all his pictures in a photographic register. Sadly, the register is now missing. Sufficient numbered prints do survive for the register to be partly reconstructed and from this we know that Carroll took nearly 3,000 pictures during his photographic career. He employed the wet collodion process which required all his glass-plates to be developed at the time the pictures were taken. Later, prints from the glass-plates were produced, often several being made. The consecutive print numbers, written neatly in Carroll's hand on the back of the photographs in the top right corner, help us to see how his photographic career developed.

Item 39b

Carroll's photographs are mainly portraits. He took pictures of his family, friends, colleagues at Christ Church, and, when the opportunity arose, celebrities of his day. He took some landscapes, a few pictures of skeletons, photographs of art-works, including paintings and sculpture, and many fine pictures of children in a wide range of different attitudes. Contrary to established opinion, he took photographs of boys as well as girls, although pictures of girls predominate.

Carroll's photographic portraits are usually in sharp focus with his sitters generally free from movement during the long exposure times which could be anything from ten to forty seconds, depending on the brightness of the daylight. Most photographs were taken outdoors, but furniture and plain backdrops using sheets created the illusion of interiors. Carroll achieved high-quality photographs by using a number of clever techniques. For a start, he tried to make sure that his sitter was comfortable and in an easy repose. He placed children in the corner of a room if standing, or wedged them into the arms of a chair if seated. He liked to have children lie on a sofa, resting their heads on pillows. He never used artificial clamps to keep his sitters still, as some photographers did, but he rested accessories, for example the tip of a violin bow, against a back wall. He studied the work of painters to find natural arrangements for hands. He kept the attention of his "photographic victims," as he called them, by storytelling and delightful conversation. For children, he made sure that the experience of having their photograph taken was a pleasant and even exciting event.

Carroll understood the pitfalls of the photographic process and had his share of failures. The wet collodion process was intricate and fraught with difficulties; chemicals sometime failed, dust or rain could easily spoil the prepared plates, and timing exposures was not a precise art. He knew that taking a successful photograph required good cooperation between the photographer and the photographed. His humorous account, "A Photographer's Day Out," expresses wonderfully the difficulties in getting good pictures, as this extract will show:

> Picture 3.—17th sitting. Placed the baby in profile. After waiting till the usual kicking had subsided, uncovered the lens. The little wretch instantly threw its head back.... This, of course; gave *two* eyes in the result, something that might be called a nose, and an unnaturally wide mouth.

14   A PHOTOGRAPHER'S DAY OUT.

PICTURE 3.—17th sitting. Placed the baby in profile. After waiting till the usual kicking had subsided, uncovered the lens. The little wretch instantly threw its head back, luckily only an inch, as it was stopped by the nurse's nose, establishing the infant's claim to " first blood" (to use a sporting phrase). This, of course; gave *two* eyes in the result, something that might be called a nose, and an unnaturally wide mouth. Called it a full-face accordingly and went on to
PICTURE 4.—The three younger girls, as they would have appeared, if by any possibility a black dose could have been administered to each of them at the same moment, and the three tied together by the hair before the expression produced

This photographic story by Carroll was published in *The South Shields Amateur Magazine* in 1860. It is an extremely rare item with only a handful of copies known to have survived, one of which is item 30 in this exhibition.

Carroll was constantly promoting his photography. He often wrote to parents suggesting they bring their children to be photographed, or asking for an introduction to another family with children he admired. He prepared a number of photographic albums to show potential sitters the range and quality of his work and, in 1872, he persuaded the college authorities to let him build a photographic studio on the roof above his rooms at Christ Church. As time went on he devoted himself more and more to portraits of children. Perhaps his favorite sitter was Alexandra "Xie" Kitchin whom he photographed at least

50 times over a period of 12 years and whose picture is included in this exhibition [Item 38]. But in 1880, after 24 years of very active photography, Carroll packed away his equipment for good and gave up "his one recreation." Writers and biographers have often speculated about what caused him to give up his hobby, and many reasons have been proposed. In a previously unpublished letter to Mrs. Hunt dated December 8, 1881, over a year after ceasing his photographic activity, he gave his own reasons:

> The last photograph I took was in August, 1880! Not one have I done this year: as there was no subject tempting enough to make me face the labour of getting the studio into working order again.... It is a very tiring amusement, & anything which can be equally well, or better, done in a professional studio for a few shillings I would always rather have so done than go through the labour myself.

This letter, which gives clear and valid reasons for leaving his photographic equipment in storage, is exhibited here for the first time [Item 32].

Even though Carroll ceased photography on his own, he still asked other people (Miss E. Gertrude Thomson, for example) to take photographs on his behalf, or he took children to professional photographers to have their picture taken. He was clearly weary of the task of getting his equipment ready for the wet collodion process. Dry-plate photography was readily available in the 1870s, and although Carroll thought it an inferior process, he recognized the advantages of having several pictures taken in a short space of time. Some writers have suggested that his "nude studies" of children gave rise to unpleasant rumors, causing him to give up photography, but this is unlikely as he continued to draw nude sketches of children. Parents (such as the Hendersons and Hatches) were usually instrumental in getting him to take photographs of their daughters naked, an activity which he saw as artistic in a spiritual and aesthetic sense. He took the Victorian view that naked children were close to angels and personified purity and godliness.

Other writers have suggested that ill-health played a part in Carroll putting photography aside. From time to time, Carroll did suffer feverish colds and, on occasion, was confined to his bed or sofa but, in general, his health was good as demonstrated by the occasional walk of 20 miles or more. Another speculation was that the chemicals used in the wet collodion process affected him, but it is now believed they did not have any particular side-effects. Another reason may have been his need to find time for other projects; he gave up his mathematics lectureship in 1881 with the express purpose of devoting more of his time to writing.

By the time Carroll put his camera away for good, his photographic reputation was already assured. The photographs selected for this exhibition demonstrate his photographic art most clearly, and help to explain why Carroll is now regarded as one of the most important amateur photographers of the Victorian era and the period's finest photographer of children.

ITEMS EXHIBITED

30) *"A Photographer's Day Out."* **By Lewis Carroll.**
THE SOUTH SHIELDS AMATEUR MAGAZINE, **Consisting Of Original Articles, In Prose And Verse, By Amateurs In South Shields And The Neighbourhood. Published In Aid Of The Building Fund Of The South Shields Mechanics' Institute, 1860 (pp. 12-16). In original pink wrappers.**

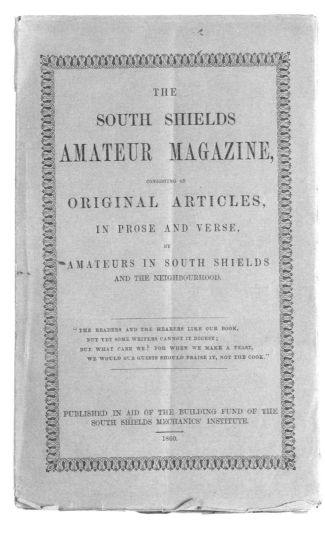

Carroll was a staunch supporter of Mechanics' Institutes. He sent them copies of several of his books, often with a presentation stamp and special binding.

Carroll's story in the magazine is narrated by a Mr. Tubbs, an amateur photographer, who is asked to photograph the family of a friend. The story reveals the difficulties of transporting the bottles of photographic chemicals and glass-plates, all very breakable. Tubbs has his heart set on taking a portrait of the beautiful Amelia, but is required to take a picture of a nearby cottage before she will give him a sitting. But trespassing on the farmer's land in order to get a good view of the cottage leads to an unceremonious and bruised conclusion to his photographic commission.

31) C. L. Dodgson to Mrs. Alice Maud Kitchin. Autograph letter signed. February 1, 1879.

Mrs. Kitchin was the mother of a favorite photographic model, Alexandra "Xie" Kitchin. In this letter, Carroll shows his concern for his photographic sitters and he asks permission to give copies of photographs of Xie to an artist, Arthur Burdett Frost, who was then illustrating Carroll's book *Rhyme? and Reason?* (1883) and would later provide pictures for *A Tangled Tale* (1885). Carroll was aware of the sensitivity of giving his photographs to someone unknown to the Kitchin's as some show Xie only partly dressed. Nevertheless, he selected six of his best which he wanted to give to Frost and sent them to Mrs. Kitchin for approval.

32) C. L. Dodgson to Mrs. Hunt. Autograph letter signed. December 8, 1881. Previously unpublished.

Christ Church, Oxford
December 8, 1881

Dear Mrs. Hunt,

As you kindly said, in your letter of Nov. 2, that you were in no immediate hurry for the Japanese things, & as I was constantly busy just then, I put the letter aside: & now I must apologize for having been so long in carrying out your wishes. I have just packed them (the things, not the wishes) & will leave them at 3, Keble Terrace.

The last photograph I took was in August, 1880! Not one have I done this year: as there was no subject tempting enough to make me face the labour of getting the studio into working order again. As to the subject <u>you</u> kindly propose to bring me each year, I hope you won't mind my saying 'Please <u>don't!</u>' Such subjects require <u>instantaneous</u> photography, which you can get to perfection at many photographers: I don't attempt that process at all. Consequently the <u>lowest</u> age that I undertake is 6 or 7 & then only girls: & even then I don't the least care to do the dress of ordinary life. It is a very tiring amusement, & anything which can be equally well, or better, done in a professional studio for a few shillings I would always rather have so done than go through the labour myself. Don't think me <u>very</u> lazy in the matter! Remember I have had 22 years of it, & have done thousands of negatives.

Believe me sincerely yours,
C.L. Dodgson

This letter sheds great light on Carroll's own reasons for giving up photography after years of speculation by his biographers and critics.

33) Photograph of Alice Liddell by Lewis Carroll. Summer 1858.

      Alice Liddell, Carroll's child-muse, photographed as "Beggar-Maid," probably the best-known photograph by Carroll. The picture was taken during the summer of 1858 in the Deanery Garden, Christ Church. The print number 354 appears in Carroll's hand on the verso of this trimmed picture made into a carte de visite. Many copies of this photograph were made, appearing in some of Carroll's own albums and also in one of Reginald Southey's. There are loose prints of this image among the Liddell photographs at Christ Church and also, as here, in a private collection. Carroll took two photographs of Alice Liddell dressed as a beggar; an earlier one taken in 1856 or 1857 was much admired by Alfred Tennyson.

34) Photograph of Twyford School boys and the headmaster, George William Kitchin by Lewis Carroll. Summer 1859.

George William Kitchin, headmaster of Twyford School, Hampshire, with the "first class" of nine pupils. The photograph was probably taken during the summer of 1859. Carroll's *Diaries* are missing for this period but the print number 394 helps to confirm the date. Carroll's younger brother, Edwin, age 13, entered Twyford School in April 1858 and may be in this photograph along with Alice Liddell's older brother Edward Henry, "Harry", age 12, but neither can be positively identified. Many other photographs were taken of the pupils and staff at Twyford School during this visit by Carroll. This particular photograph is included in the Kitchin family album (which is in the Lindseth Collection) containing many other photographs by Carroll.

35) Photograph of Lewis Carroll and the MacDonald family. July 1863.

This is one of two known copies of this photograph showing Carroll and the MacDonalds, photographed in the garden of the MacDonald home, Elm Lodge, Hampstead, London. The picture was taken in July 1863, and shows Mrs. Louisa MacDonald, Greville, Mary, Lewis Carroll, Irene and Caroline. The print is unnumbered but is around number 1000. Suggestions have been made that Carroll took the photograph using a piece of cotton or string attached to the lens-cap. However, the sharpness of the image and the lack of evidence for the cotton or string indicates that someone else "took" the photograph, probably Mr. MacDonald, although the arrangement was certainly organized by Carroll himself. Carroll was a long-time friend of the MacDonalds. George MacDonald was a writer whom Carroll admired. They both suffered from a speech hesitation and met in 1860 at speech therapy sessions with Dr. Hunt at Ore, near Hastings. (See page 54 for illustration.)

36) Photograph of Greville MacDonald by Lewis Carroll. July 31, 1863.

Greville MacDonald, age seven, standing next to a statue, photographed on July 31, 1863, at Elm Lodge. The print number is 1029. Carroll first met Greville and his sister Mary at the studio of the sculptor, Alexander Munro. When Carroll lent a draft of the manuscript of *Alice's Adventures Under Ground* to the MacDonalds, so that Mrs. MacDonald could read the story to her children, it was Greville MacDonald who exclaimed "there should be sixty-thousand copies!" This is said to have been Carroll's inspiration to have *Alice's Adventures in Wonderland* published.

37) Photograph of Elizabeth "Beta" Thresher by Lewis Carroll. September 9 or 10, 1875.

Carroll first met the Thresher children, Elizabeth, Mabel and Mary, at Sandown, Isle of Wight, in September 1874. Their father, Rev. James Hanville Thresher, MA, New College, Oxford, was a teacher at Twyford School at the time that Carroll's two brothers, Skeffington and Wilfred, were pupils there. In 1874 he held a curacy at Winchester. Carroll took this photograph on either September 9 or 10, 1875, on a visit to the Threshers at their home in Winchester. Here, Beta is dressed up as a Spanish lady. The print number is unknown but must be between 2374 and 2403.

38) **a.** **Glass-plate negative of Alexandra "Xie" Kitchin as "Penelope Boothby" by Lewis Carroll. July 1, 1876. Number 2423.**

b. **Also displayed is a modern print from the negative.**

c. ***SORROWS. SACRED TO THE MEMORY OF PENELOPE.* [By Brooke Boothby] London: W. Bulmer and Co., 1796.**

This may be
Lewis Carroll's
fingerprint.

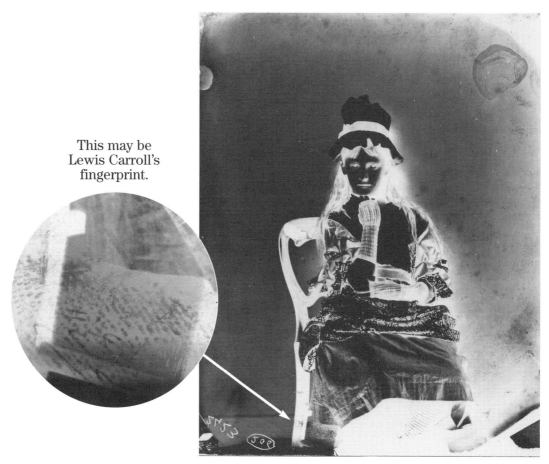

Item 38a

Alexandra "Xie" Kitchin as "Penelope Boothby" was photographed by Carroll on July 1, 1876. Xie is posed in the attitude and costume of "Penelope" as depicted in Sir Joshua Reynolds' famous portrait, made into a mezzotint by Samuel Cousins and published in *Sorrows. Sacred to the Memory of Penelope*, 1796. Shown here is the original glass-plate negative. These glass negatives are rare for two reasons: many were cleaned and recycled by Carroll, and others were subsequently broken. Fingerprints can be seen on the glass-plate along the lower edge. These may be Carroll's.

Henry Holiday, illustrator and himself a sitter for Carroll's camera, was once asked by Carroll if he "knew how to get excellence in a photograph." Holiday was forced to admit defeat, to which Carroll replied in typical witty fashion, using a clever play on words: "Take a lens and put Xie before it."

Item 38b

The Sir Joshua Reynolds engraving of Penelope. This was parodied by Carroll for the photograph.

Item 38c

39) The versos of two photographs by Lewis Carroll with his autograph inscriptions in purple ink.

a. "for Alexandra Kitchin, from Lewis Carroll. Sep. 10. 1873."

Alexandra "Xie" Kitchin had been Carroll's favorite photographic model for nearly four years by the time this picture was given to her, which makes it rather unusual that Carroll should sign it with his pseudonym rather than his real name. His usual method of inscribing a photograph was to sign it "from the Artist," as shown in the next item. This inscribed photograph probably resulted from a personal request as indicated in a letter from Carroll to Xie written on August 21, 1873, and it may have been her wish to receive a photograph from "Lewis Carroll." Such an inscription on the back of a photograph is rare.

b. "given to Dolly Draper by the Artist. Jan. 24/77."
   Print number 2445.

Carroll's usual method of inscribing a photograph was to refer to himself as the "Artist." This is a clear indication that he saw his photographic activities as artistic rather than in any sense a practical or scientific pastime. In many respects photography was his substitute for artistic competence in drawing, a skill he felt he lacked. In all his photographs, he took great pains to ensure that the final photographic image was aesthetically pleasing to the eye in both form and composition. He studied the work of great artists in order to learn from their techniques of composition, and this he recreated in his photographs, paying particular attention to the position of hands and to the attitude of his sitters.

40) Photograph of Lewis Carroll by Oscar G. Rejlander. March 28, 1863.

Oscar Gustave Rejlander (1813-75), who was born in Sweden, married an English woman and settled in Lincoln, making his living as a portrait painter. He took up photography in 1853, and in 1860 moved to London where he worked as a professional photographer until his death. His reputation as a photographer was made with his portraits and nude studies of women and children. Carroll paid a visit to Rejlander's studio on March 28, 1863, noting in his *Diary*: "I found Rejlander at home, and got my picture taken, large and small, half length." This is an example of the small, carte de visite portrait of Carroll taken by Rejlander showing Carroll sitting with a camera lens in hand which he is cleaning. The pose is confident and reveals the sense of pleasure that photography brought to Carroll.

This photograph is the cover illustration.

VI

"Are You Kissable?"

By Morton N. Cohen

"You must remember this:
A kiss is just a kiss...."
—Herman Hupfeld, "As Time Goes By"

We are not Victorians, and according to the calendar, we are a century away from our nineteenth-century predecessors. But psychologically, and perhaps spiritually, light years separate us. This enormous distance is the product of the tremendous strides the world has taken since the invention of the airplane, the motor car, radio and television, satellites for exploring space, computers, fax machines, and in developing a myriad of medical treatments. What is more, our distance from the Victorians is just as great in beliefs, in feelings, in understanding, and most especially in attitudes. Perhaps our greatest difference from the Victorians is reflected in our attitudes towards children.

Although child prostitution thrived in nineteenth-century England, educated and respectable Victorians, those who belonged to what they called "polite Society," cherished childhood deeply. Well-bred Victorians saw the works of Rousseau, Blake, Wordsworth, Coleridge and Dickens as their inheritance, and those writers sang the praises of the child as no other artists had done before. To the romantic view of the child, the Victorians added a cupful of sentimentality and another cupful of religious reverence. The upshot was that they treasured the child's purity and innocence; they saw children as angelic messengers from God. We need only look at the illustrations in newspapers, magazines, novels, or at the drawings and paintings of the time, to see how Victorians idealized the child, both dressed and undressed. Indeed, those with aesthetic credentials, artistic aspirations, sensitive natures – all qualities embodied in Charles Dodgson – virtually quivered with excitement in the presence of children. They worshipped at the shrine of childhood.

One of his young friends tells us that Dodgson devoted three-fourths of his life to his child-friends. He did all he could for them. For him, these friendships were enormously serious relationships. As a clergyman, he was beyond reproach, and believing that his pursuit of these children was thoroughly innocent (and, mind you, we have no proof that it was anything but innocent), he was free to seek friendships with children. He garnered a huge amount of pleasure from these friendships, but he also gave a great deal. In fact, he did everything he could for these young friends. He took them on railway journeys, on outings to the theater, to art galleries, and he went with them on long walks.

He fed them, he gave them inscribed copies of his books, he sent them presents, he paid for some of their lessons in French, art and singing, and he even paid some dentist bills. He entertained them in his rooms at Christ Church, he took them to visit his family home in Guildford, he treated them to seaside holidays at Eastbourne. He wrote poems with their names built into the verses, he dedicated his books to them, he wrote them amusing and loving letters, he taught them logic, he gave them spiritual guidance. He held their hands, he sat some of them on his knee, he cuddled them, and he was, with the consent of their parents, on "kissing terms" with gaggles of these young girls at various times. He made sketches of them, and he photographed them, sometimes in the nude, again only with their own and their parents' consent.

Although we today would never countenance such behavior, Dodgson kissed away happily for years. His kisses were not only condoned; they were often returned. He was occasionally rebuffed, as when, as he tells it himself, an eight-year old American "declined to be kissed on wishing goodbye, on the ground that she 'never kissed gentlemen.' It is rather painful," Dodgson adds, "to see the lovely simplicity of childhood so soon rubbed off: but I fear it is true that there are no children in America."

You and I know that Dodgson could not behave today as he did in his time. But in an age when emotions were guarded and repressed, the tall, erect, soft-spoken Charles Dodgson could bend over to hug and kiss a young girl, to show her that she was cared for, that she was loved, that she mattered. Our twentieth-century awareness, our suspicions, our Freudian analysis condemns such relationships and makes even mothers and fathers self-conscious about touching, let alone kissing, their very own children. But I wonder if we are better off now in spite of our modern awareness.

We believe as we do because we are more self-conscious, perhaps more knowledgeable, about the workings of the mind, about the unconscious, about what we call our psyches, and about our deep-seated motives. But are we wiser? Are we and our children better off because we hold back the friendly hand, the gentle lip? Whither has fled the old innocence? Why do we thwart our instincts, why do we read harsh meanings into our natural attempts at intimacy?

Why is a kiss no longer just a kiss?

ITEMS EXHIBITED

41) C. L. Dodgson to Mrs. Alice Maud Kitchin. Autograph letter signed. February 12, 1880.

Dodgson wrote this letter to Mrs. Kitchin hoping she could repair his breach with Mrs. Owen as a result of his kissing her daughter "Atty." He wrote:

> If ever you should, in the course of conversation with Mrs. Owen, touch on the subject of the angry correspondence just concluded, I hope you will sooth [*sic*] her feelings, and get her to consent to forgive me at some future time (say 5 years hence). And though I fear the children will *never* be allowed to enter my rooms again, perhaps she might be got to allow them to recognise me in the street? At present I really don't know *what* would result from a chance meeting. I think I should cross the road if I saw them coming, and so avoid the difficulty!

On February 5, 1880, Dodgson "brought in 'Atty' Owen and her brother in my rooms" to wait for their father, another Christ Church don. "She does not look 14 yet," Dodgson wrote in his *Diary*, the age at which, by convention, kissing had to stop, "and when, having kissed her in parting, I learned (from Owen) that she is 17, I was astonished, but I don't think either of us was much displeased at the mistake having been made." Mrs. Owen, however, was outraged when she learned of the incident.

42) C. L. Dodgson to Mrs. Alice Maud Kitchin. Autograph letter signed. February 24, 1880.

Dodgson continued to write to Mrs. Kitchin to inform her of developments in the "Atty Owen affair."

> I met Mr. O., and Atty, on my staircase a day or two
> ago, and shook hands with *her* and interchanged a remark
> on the weather with him. A sort of "armed peace," I take it.

Dodgson's charade, on the verso of this letter, is illustrated here and the answer is **Atty Owen**. Here is how one arrives at it:

First: The letter **a** is the first in the word **all** and so heads it.
Next: The letter **t** tends to finish the word **it**.
Third: The letters **ow** are in the word **Town**.
Fourth: The letters **en** are at the beginning of the word **ending**.
Whole: Combine the sounds and we get: **Atty Owen**.

43) C. L. Dodgson to Mr. A. H. J. Greenidge. Autograph letter signed. May 24, 1895.

Edith Lucy's fiancé had written to Dodgson telling him of Edith's suggestion that they stop kissing and Dodgson agreed to the "wise suggestion." Dodgson wrote:

> I would like you to know, from myself, how <u>entirely</u> I approve of Edith's wise suggestion that she & I had better now drop the "kissing" which used to mark our greetings. It is a real pleasure to me to feel that, in carrying out her suggestion, I am doing what will I hope be satisfactory to one she loves so well.

Edith Lucy was 24 years old at the time. She had been one of Dodgson's students when he gave logic classes at the Oxford High School for Girls. She had recently become engaged to A. H. J. Greenidge, another Oxford don, whom she married on June 29.

44) C. L. Dodgson to Mrs. Bessie Hatch. Autograph letter signed. Undated. Previously unpublished.

Dodgson appeals to Mrs. Hatch to invent a "symbol" which a young girl could wear to indicate if she is of "kissable" age.

Dear Mrs. Hatch:

   You would do a good service for old bachelors like me, if you would invent a symbol (say a locket or ribbon) which should indicate, as to any young lady, whether one is expected to kiss or shake hands. My doubt just now is as to B., it is so long since I have been in your house. So, unless she takes the initiative, I shall only shake hands.
   The difficulty is constantly occurring to me, & I can't discover <u>any</u> rule among my friends. Even in the Oxford High School I have 2 young friends, aged 15 and 17, who expect me to kiss them: & outside it the same law prevails with friends up to 19, & even up to 24 or so! Anything over <u>20</u> I still regard as abnormal: but I am now so old that all under 20 seem 'children' to me, & I adopt any salutation they choose.

Believe me
Sincerely yours
C. L. Dodgson

   Dodgson was a friend of the Hatch family for more than 25 years. He photographed the children, gave them inscribed copies of his books, visited them often, took them on outings, and helped to advance their careers. The father of the family was Edwin Hatch, a theologian and Vice-Principal of St. Mary's Hall, Oxford. Dodgson dubbed the three daughters **BEE**, shorthand for **B**eatrice, **E**thel and **E**velyn.

**45) C. L. Dodgson to Isa Bowman. Autograph letter signed.
April 14, 1890.**

This is Dodgson's best known "kissing" letter. Isa Bowman had offered to give him millions of hugs and kisses and in this response he does a mathematical calculation to determine how long it will take.

"Among the celebrated theatrical families who from their childhood upwards have been cherished by the play-going public none have filled a more prominent position for the last decade that the Bowman sisters," wrote a critic in *Era* on June 14, 1902. Dodgson had a good deal to do with putting that family on the stage and with shaping its success. He first encountered Isa, who had a small part in the original stage production of *Alice*, in 1886, and subsequently met the other Bowman children, three younger sisters and a brother. With Dodgson's help, all went on to act professionally – the girls to full-time stage careers. Isa acted the leading role in the 1888 revival of *Alice*. Dodgson dedicated *Sylvie and Bruno* to her.

VII
Lewis Carroll, Bibliophile

By Jeffrey Stern

Carroll's library was entirely formed by him and he was rather proud of it. It was scattered at auction shortly after his death in 1898 so that apart from a few known surviving books, such as those displayed here, all we now know about it comes from the original estate auction catalogue and the catalogues issued by the booksellers who attended the sale. Yet it is clear that it was in Carroll's very nature to build a library and the surviving photographs of his Christ Church rooms show that they were dominated by bookcases. Nevertheless the fact that he was a true bibliophile, an avid collector and an active reader of other people's books, has often been overlooked by his biographers. His life was, in truth, absolutely walled in by books, as a writer, publisher, reader and collector – yet this is a fact so obvious that it is easily missed. He was even, for a time, a Sub-Librarian at Christ Church, taking up this appointment in 1855. Books were the biggest thing in his life – a fact that he himself acknowledged as actually a sadness; when he wrote to his Uncle Skeffington for a camera it was, according to his own words in his *Diary* (January 22, 1856), because at Christ Church, "I want some occupation here than mere reading and writing." Of course, this is not to deny that a great deal of his energy was also given to teaching, college life, theater, art, child-friends, photography, family duties and so on. Yet the truth remains that he spent most of his life alone, in his rooms, in Tom Quad doing "mere reading and writing," surrounded by books.

There is also some evidence from his *Diary* that Carroll actively sought out bookshops. The *Diary* includes numerous descriptions of Carroll's reading and self-improvement schemes, as he spurred himself on to both deeper and wider intellectual endeavor. In short, the library was Carroll's lifeline; it broke his solitude, it occupied his days and the continual and gradual accretion of books gave him another useful self-imposed task that could never actually be completed. Most of all, the library fired his own imagination and gave his energies endless space; it was a place in which to relax and a place to read. Its formation was an honorable and traditional occupation for a gentleman-scholar – and Carroll reveled in it.

When, however, the bibliophile of today surveys Carroll's library, it often seems disappointing because it has very few books that would now be classed as antiquarian and of high individual quality. In fact his library does show that he was, in a small way, a deliberate collector of rare books. Among these are Dickens' *A Christmas Carol* (reproduction of the author's original manuscript); a facsimile reprint of the first edition of *Robinson Crusoe*; a facsimile of the first edition of Milton's *Paradise Lost*; and three rare Keats first editions. The preponderance of facsimile printings here might suggest that Carroll agreed with the sensible notion, then prevalent among collectors, that the original appearance of a text was an important element in the understanding of its true meaning. This would certainly harmonize with his own extreme care about how his own publications actually looked. It was from his own library that Carroll would have gained the taste, knowledge and experience to fight his publisher, printer and illustrators – ironically to create one of the greatest prizes for bibliophiles, the 1865 *Alice*.

By far the majority of Carroll's books were not trophies from the past, but were systematically accumulated for his use. In a real way this makes their range and quantity even more extraordinary. When intact, his library may have been 3,000 volumes strong – certainly a large private library. In preparing my book, *Lewis Carroll, Bibliophile* (Lewis Carroll Society, 1997), I identified 2,231 books (not including duplicates) and was able to demonstrate with great clarity just what Carroll's main interests were, especially when the subjects were ranked in order of his holdings in each subject. Thus literature (711); theology (305); children's books (154); and mathematics (117) were the clear and obvious favorites, but history (110); medicine (88 titles – even after many were given away to his nephew); language (82); and science (70) were also strongly represented, whilst Carroll's travel and topography (115) might be seen as a surprise – for a man who travelled abroad only once. Other surprises were, clearly, his comparatively large number of books on the occult (32) and women (29).

46) *WUTHERING HEIGHTS* **By Ellis Bell [Emily Brontë]; And**
AGNES GREY, **By Acton Bell [Anne Brontë]; With A** *PREFACE,*
AND MEMOIR OF BOTH AUTHORS, **By Currer Bell [Charlotte**
Brontë]. A New Edition. London: Smith, Elder and Co., 1860.
Two volumes.

With Carroll's typical ownership initials interlaced and in purple ink on the title page. Of *Wuthering Heights,* Carroll remarked in his *Diary*: "Finished that extraordinary book. It is of all the novels I ever read the one I should least like to be a character in myself. All the 'dramatis personae' are so unusual and unpleasant. The only failure in the book is the writing it in the person of a gentleman. Heathcliff and Catherine are original and most powerfully drawn idealities: one cannot believe that such human beings ever existed: they have far more of the fiend in them. The vision at the beginning is I think the finest piece of writing in the book." This book was lot 651 in the Dodgson estate sale catalogue.

WUTHERING HEIGHTS

BY ELLIS BELL;

AND

AGNES GREY,

BY ACTON BELL;

WITH A

PREFACE, AND MEMOIR OF BOTH AUTHORS,

BY CURRER BELL,

AUTHOR OF " JANE EYRE," " SHIRLEY," " VILLETTE," " THE PROFESSOR," ETC.

A NEW EDITION.

LONDON:
SMITH, ELDER AND CO., 65, CORNHILL.
1860.

47) *THE POETICAL WORKS OF PERCY BYSSHE SHELLEY.*
Edited By Mrs. Shelley. London: Edward Moxon, 1839.
Three volumes.

Inscribed on the half-title of volume one: "For John George Perry Esq
from M W Shelley," and on the verso of the upper free endpaper, inscribed with
Carroll's ownership initials. An interesting example of Carroll collecting an
association copy – this is a superbly evocative inscribed set from the editor and
wife of the poet, Mary Wollstonecraft Shelley (the daughter of Mary
Wollstonecraft and William Godwin) – herself the author of the classic Gothic
novel *Frankenstein,* a copy of which Carroll also had in his library. This book
was lot 353 in the Dodgson estate sale where it brought £1/10/0.

48) *THE PICTORIAL BOOK OF ANCIENT BALLAD POETRY OF GREAT BRITAIN, HISTORICAL, TRADITIONAL AND ROMANTIC*. J. S. Moore, Editor. London: Bell and Daldy, 1860.

A finely bound copy given to Carroll by his close and oldest friend, Thomas Vere Bayne (one of two witnesses to Carroll's will), inscribed by Carroll in black ink on the upper free endpaper: "Charles L. Dodgson from T. V. B. Ch[rist] Ch[urch], March 1860." Carroll was 28 years old at the time. This book was part of lot 390 in the Dodgson estate sale catalogue. Carroll's knowledge of early English poetry was surprisingly extensive and it is well represented in his library. Cultured Victorians were drawn to the medieval period as evidence of an inspiring golden chivalric age, and this became part of the Pre-Raphaelite vision lasting right up to the end of the century with William Morris and the Gothic revival. Amongst others, Carroll's White Knight, Ye Carpette Knyghte, and Hatta and Haigha (with their "Anglo-Saxon attitudes") can all be traced to this enthusiasm. Indeed, the sound of "Jabberwocky" itself is in parody of pre-Chaucerian poetry.

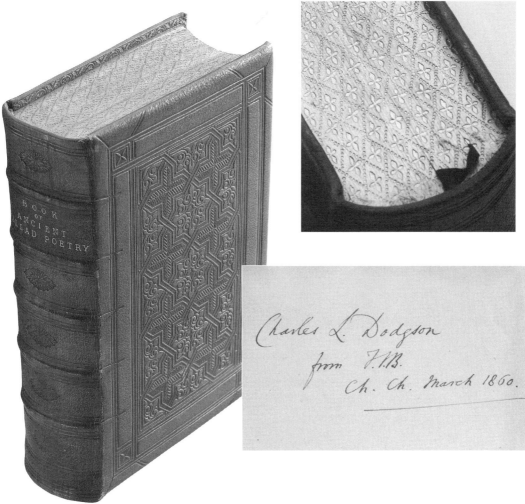

Ch. Ch.
June 27 / 9³

My dear Butler,
    Many thanks - But
please inscribe it
as your gift! An
inscribed book is
54.37 as valuable
to me as one without
an inscription.

Very sincerely yrs,
    C. L. Dodgson.

Item 49

VIII

"An inscribed book is 54.37 as valuable to me...."

By Jon A. Lindseth

Lewis Carroll was a bibliophile, so it was important that when an author presented him with a book, it was inscribed. When his Oxford colleague, Arthur G. Butler, gave him a copy of his latest book uninscribed, Carroll actually returned it with the note: "Many thanks, but please inscribe it as your gift! An inscribed book is 54.37 as valuable to me as one without an inscription" [Item 49].

It is virtually certain that Lewis Carroll inscribed every book of his that he gave away – and it is known that he gave away an enormous number. The Carroll scholar, Edward Wakeling, is in the process of compiling a census of all books inscribed by Carroll. To date he has identified over 1000.

Carroll himself probably kept a list (now lost) of the books he inscribed and their recipients, since he was a meticulous record keeper. For example, he kept records of his dinner guests, whom they sat next to, and what they were served. His letter register, which he started the month before his twenty-ninth birthday, had 98,721 entries at the time of his death. However, the records of his inscribed books that do survive are very few. We do know the names of the 69 to whom he inscribed his 1866 edition of *Alice*, as he listed them in his *Diary*. Of these books, 44 went to girls and women, 20 to men, three to couples, one to his family at Croft Rectory, and one to the Senior Common Room at Christ Church. The copies inscribed to two of the girls, Edith Denman and Katie Brine, are now in my collection.

Of the men who received a copy, it is not surprising that one went to his publisher, Alexander Macmillan, and one to his illustrator, John Tenniel. He also sent a copy to the poet, Alfred Tennyson, and another to the German publisher of English literature, Baron Tauchnitz, although Tauchnitz never published any of Carroll's books.

From Carroll's *Diary* of December 8, 1871, we know that he inscribed 101 copies of *Through the Looking-Glass* "Christmas 1871," but here we find no record of the names. My associate, Bea Sidaway, is attempting to compile a census of these and to date has identified 60. I have five of them in my collection.

We also know from Carroll's *Diary* that on September 16, 1887, he went "To Macmillan's and inscribed 41 books to go to children who had acted in *Alice*." This refers to the stage production of *Alice in Wonderland*, December 23, 1886. I have two of these, one of which is item 62 in this exhibit. For Carroll, signing his books for presentation was something of an obsession, and many more examples of this activity can be found in his *Diaries*.

Carroll did much more than send first editions inscribed at the time of publication. Often when he met an interesting new friend, usually a little girl, he followed the meeting by sending her an inscribed book. He kept a stock of books in his own library just for this purpose. His *Diary* entry of June 14,

1869, reads, "I have today sent off a copy (of *Alice*) to my railway companions of yesterday...." These were the three Drury sisters.

Most of Carroll's books are simply inscribed to the recipient "from the Author" and generally followed by the date. But he had many other forms of inscription as the 127 inscribed copies in my collection show. His *Stamp-Case* is inscribed from "the Inventor" and *Euclid Books I, II*, from "the Editor." Five of his early books are inscribed to the recipient, but not signed by him. Five are inscribed "CLD" and two "C.L. Dodgson." One copy of his *Easter Greetings* is inscribed from "the writer." Two family members received copies of his books inscribed "from his affectionate Uncle" or "from her affectionate brother."

Twelve items in my collection are inscribed "Lewis Carroll." Several are in this exhibition.

Carroll sought to be considered a visual artist as well as a literary one. He knew his drawing limitations (Ruskin confirmed this), but he knew that his photographs were significant. Four of his photographs in my collection carry the revealing inscription "from the Artist."

Carroll's artistic interests can be readily seen. For example, he personally illustrated his manuscript of *Alice's Adventures Under Ground*, and he often sent drawings as suggestions to the professional illustrators of his other books. He frequently drew pictures of little girls at the seashore and inscribed them. He was a friend of artists and often photographed their works. Lewis Carroll's fond hope to be recognized as a photographic artist has now passed the test of time. Helmut Gernsheim, an historian of early photography, called him "the most outstanding photographer of children in the nineteenth century."

While most of Carroll's inscriptions are routine, a few are very unusual and self-revealing as can be seen in the items exhibited here.

ITEMS EXHIBITED

49) C. L. Dodgson to Arthur G. Butler. Autograph letter signed. June 27, 1893. Previously unpublished.

Christ Church
June 27, 1893

My dear Butler,

Many thanks. But please inscribe it as your gift! An inscribed book is 54.37 as valuable to me as one without an inscription.

Very sincerely yours,
C. L. Dodgson

An illuminating letter both concerning Carroll as a book collector and as a giver of his own books. He obviously thought that to receive an uninscribed book from an author was a great pity – a fault of which he himself was never guilty. Arthur Butler published five literary books. It is probable, because of the date, that the book to which this letter refers was *Harold. A Drama in Four Acts*, 1892. Indeed, the book survived in Carroll's library and is listed as part of lot 858 in the Carroll estate sale catalogue. Unfortunately, it is not noted in the catalogue whether Butler actually did inscribe it.

50) *ALICE'S ADVENTURES UNDER GROUND.* **By Lewis Carroll.
London and New York: Macmillan and Co., 1886.**

Inscribed by Lewis Carroll in purple ink on the half-title:

> To Her, whose children's smiles fed the narrator's fancy
> and were his rich reward: from the Author. Xmas. 1886

Undoubtedly one of the most poignant inscriptions ever written by Carroll. This copy was given to Mrs. Lorina Liddell, the wife of Dean Henry Liddell of Christ Church, and the mother of Alice. Another copy of this book, given to Alice herself, is now in the Christ Church library and contains this inscription:

> To Her, whose namesake one happy summer's day
> inspired this story: from the Author. Xmas. 1886

51) A hand-drawn board by Carroll for the game *Nine Men's Morris*.

Inscribed by Lewis Carroll in black ink on the verso:

Olive Butler, from the White Knight. Nov. 21, 1892.

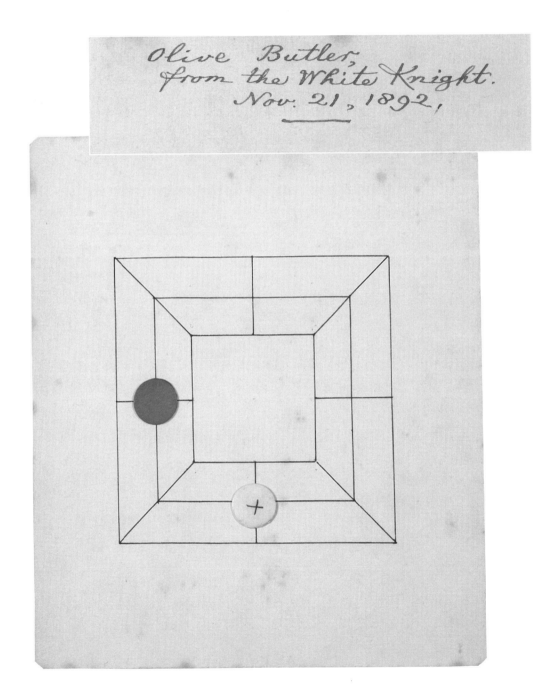

This ancient game is mentioned by Shakespeare in *Measure for Measure* in Act 1, Scene 2.

There has been a long-standing debate as to just who was the model for the White Knight; some say Tenniel, others Dodgson. And some have said the White Knight drawing was Tenniel's parody of Dodgson, even though Tenniel clearly portrayed himself as the White Knight in at least two later drawings. But the frontispiece of the White Knight in *Through the Looking-Glass* is, after all, only an illustration of Carroll's story. The greater issue is, who did Carroll have in mind as the original for the White Knight when he wrote the story? This self-revealing inscription resolves that question once and for all.

It should be recalled that Carroll described Alice's farewell encounter with his persona, the White Knight, in the following melancholy way:

> So saying, he [the White Knight] stopped his horse and let the reins fall on its neck: then, slowly beating time with one hand, and with a faint smile lighting up his gentle foolish face, as if he enjoyed the music of his song, he began.
>
> Of all the strange things that Alice saw in her journey Through the Looking-Glass this was the one that she always remembered most clearly. Years afterward she could bring the whole scene back again, as if it had been only yesterday – the mild blue eyes and kindly smile of the Knight – the setting sun gleaming through his hair, and shining on his armour in a blaze of light that quite dazzled her –.
>
> As the Knight sang the last words of the ballad, he gathered up the reins, and turned his horse's head along the road by which they had come. "You've only a few yards to go," he said, "down the hill and over that little brook, and then you'll be a Queen – But you'll stay and see me off first?" he added as Alice turned with an eager look in the direction to which he pointed. "I shan't be long. You'll wait and wave your handkerchief when I get to that turn in the road? I think it'll encourage me, you see."
>
> "Of course I'll wait," said Alice: "and thank you very much for coming so far – and for the song – I liked it very much."
>
> "I hope so," the Knight said doubtfully: "but you didn't cry so much as I thought you would."
>
> So they shook hands, and then the Knight rode slowly away into the forest.
>
> *Through the Looking-Glass*, Chapter VIII.

52) *PHANTASMAGORIA AND OTHER POEMS.* **By Lewis Carroll. London: Macmillan and Co., 1869.**

Inscribed by Lewis Carroll in purple ink on the half-title.

Presented to
Lady Maud Cecil,
in ecstatic recognition
of
the overwhelming patronage which
she
has ever diffused
over Literature, Science, Art, and
other

PHANTASMAGORIA :
and in token of
a convulsive regard,
which Time has only deepened,
for
the many transcendental virtues
which
do equal Honour to
her Head
and
her Heart;
by
her grateful Servant,
the Author.

July. 1871.

This extraordinary inscription is unlike any other of Carroll's seen by this collector. It is difficult to imagine what the 13-year-old Maud Cecil or her parents thought when this book arrived.

Lady Maud Cecil was a daughter of Lord and Lady Salisbury. Carroll first met the family in June 1870, when Salisbury was installed as Chancellor of Oxford. He was later to be prime minister, and Carroll often wrote to him, suggesting policy or legislative action. The Salisburys came to Carroll's rooms to be photographed, and he was a visitor to both their London home and their country estate, Hatfield House. They remained good friends until Carroll's death.

While this inscription is obviously one of comic hyperbole, it also contains some element of Carroll's true feelings. As he wrote in his *Diary* on June 27, 1871, after he had visited the Royal Academy with Maud and her younger sister Gwendolen: "the intelligent remarks of the children added much to the interest of the exhibition."

Miss Christina Rossetti.

Item 53

IX
Lewis Carroll, Pre-Raphaelitism and Christina Rossetti

By Jeffrey Stern

Our image of the Pre-Raphaelites is that of a group of young revolutionary painters and poets, determinedly archaic at times, often libertine, immoral, and dangerously explorative. Our image of C. L. Dodgson is that of a retiring, stammering, celibate cleric, a stalwart of the English establishment. How then can Carroll be considered a Pre-Raphaelite?

One primary error in forming our image of Carroll and attempting to understand his creativity is neglecting to focus on C. L. Dodgson's most creative years – 1860 to 1876 – and even when we do so we must still be selective. His *Diaries* are a catalogue of boredom, if taken as a whole, and yet they give glimpses of extraordinary days during particular years when they show Carroll's involvement with his contemporaries, especially poets and painters. Indeed, he was as enthusiastic about the visual arts as was his heroine: "And what is the use of a book," thought Alice, "without pictures." Alice adds, of course, "or conversations"– and Carroll here too was eager, especially when the conversations were with eminent Victorians. He spoke with and watched painters as they worked, photographed original pictures, bought reproductions, gave pictures their titles, made suggestions and criticisms, and visited art schools. He knew, among others, Crane, Watts, Holman Hunt, Woolner, Collins, Leighton, Paton, Hughes, Prinsep, Munro, Doyle, Millais, Rossetti, and Ruskin. He owned prints and books about paintings, as well as original drawings and pictures. Among the latter was an important Pre-Raphaelite oil painting by Arthur Hughes, *The Lady with the Lilacs*, which was purchased in 1863 and hung in his study – and which undoubtedly influenced how he drew Alice in the original manuscript of *Alice's Adventures Under Ground*. I have already made these points in "Lewis Carroll the Pre-Raphaelite" (in *Lewis Carroll Observed*, edited by Edward Guiliano, 1976). There I put the case for Carroll's visual image of Alice as coming directly from his contact, not only with this Hughes painting, but also from his knowledge of the paintings of Dante Gabriel Rossetti.

We know of Carroll's contact with the Rossettis from his *Diaries* – that in 1863 he made several visits to Rossetti's studio. He had met the Rossettis through Alexander Munro the sculptor (and friend of George MacDonald); the first meeting is recorded in Carroll's *Diary* as having taken place on September 30th, 1863: "Called with Mr. and Mrs. Munro at Mr. Rossetti's, and saw some very lovely pictures, most of them only half finished: he was most hospitable in the offers of the use of house and garden for picture taking, and I arranged to take my camera there on Monday...."

It is clear that Carroll was primarily concerned with his own art of photographing the famous, and his glimpses of Rossetti's paintings were, at this stage, a bonus, though one which had its own effect. On the Tuesday following this entry, Carroll saw Christina and some more of Rossetti's art:

> Went over to Mr. Rossetti's, and began unpacking the camera etc. While I was doing so Miss Christina Rossetti arrived, and Mr. Rossetti introduced me to her. She seemed a little shy at first, and I had very little time for conversation with her, but I much liked what I saw of her. She sat for two pictures, Mr. Rossetti for one.... I afterwards looked through a huge volume of drawings, some of which I am to photograph, a great treat, as I had never seen such exquisite drawings before. I dined with Mr. Rossetti, and spent some of the evening there:... A memorable day....

One of Carroll's portraits of Christina is item 53, inscribed by Carroll with her name. Also included are photographs of Gabriel Rossetti and Alexander Munro, (Items 54 a & b).

Carroll was virtually unknown at this time (it was 1863; *Alice* appeared in 1865), and yet he had penetrated one of the great citadels of art in Victorian England. It would have been surprising if such an encounter had no effect on him, yet it was by no means an obvious one.

Apart from an idealized Pre-Raphaelite female face as painted by Gabriel Rossetti – what else could Carroll have found in the Rossetti household? What also in their art would have pleased him and encouraged some of his own ideas? This must surely be located in his friendship with Christina Rossetti. For she was both prudish and poetic, superlatively spiritual (Holman Hunt found her eyes the only ones he could use for the Christ in his famous picture *Light of the World*) and, sometimes, a writer for children – all of this would have appealed to Carroll. He owned copies of many of her books, including *Speaking Likenesses*, (a copy of the rare first edition with dustwrapper is exhibited here [Item 55]). This book is credited as actually being the first parody of *Alice*. It was illustrated by the very same Arthur Hughes whose painting so influenced Carroll. Carroll also owned copies of Christina Rossetti's *A Pageant and other Poems; The Prince's Progress; Verses*, 1874, (dedicated to her mother and privately printed – hence a rarity); *Sing Song* and *Goblin Market*, all in their first editions, as well as a copy of her 1894 *Verses* which was inscribed to him "from his old acquaintance the Author." (See Stern, *Lewis Carroll, Bibliophile*, pp.148-9.) He also owned a copy of her *Time Flies: A Reading Diary*, 1885, exhibited here [Item 56]. This has a card pasted to the upper paste-down with the inscription in Christina Rossetti's hand "The Rev. C. L. Dodgson from C. G. R." For his part, he presented her with copies of his books; a copy of the German *Alice* is exhibited here [Item 57], inscribed to her by Carroll. That they got on well is clear from the following letter of thanks for her copy of *Alice's Adventures in Wonderland*:

A thousand and one thanks – surely an appropriate number – for the funny pretty book you have so kindly sent me. My Mother and Sister as well as myself made ourselves quite at home yesterday in Wonderland: and (if I am not shamefully old for such an avowal) I confess it would give me sincere pleasure to fall in with that conversational rabbit, that endearing puppy, that very sparkling dormouse. Of the Hatter's acquaintance I am not ambitious, and the March Hare may fairly remain an open question. The woodcuts are charming. Have you seen the few words of strong praise already awarded to your volume by the *Reader*?

To descend to very prosy prose. Please do not forget that we are still in your debt for the last vignettes of my Sister: 9 copies, I think. Two or three months ago her carte de visite was taken at Harrogate and turned out an admirable likeness.

My Mother and Sister unite in cordial remembrances. Pray believe me very truly yours, Christina G. Rossetti, 1865.

[Dodgson family collection, 20/3].

But apart from such social compatibility with its polite expression of friendship, Carroll and Christina Rossetti had a certain artistic kinship and undoubtedly influenced each other. That she was influenced by him has been noticed before: her *Speaking Likenesses*, especially, was cited by Percy Muir (*English Children's Books*, p.153) in 1954 as being "by no means free, in either conception or illustration, from the influence of *Alice*." But Carroll, especially early on in his literary career, was not above being influenced by her and by her greatest poem, *Goblin Market*, which appeared in 1862. Carroll noted in his *Diary* for May 12th of that year:

I have been reading in these last few days, Miss Rossetti's *Goblin Market*, etc. and admire them very much.

In "these last few days" around May 12th, 1862, Carroll had also himself written a poem titled "Stolen Waters" and these two poems show fascinating similarities. Not only the style but also the mood and theme of both "Stolen Waters" and *Goblin Market* are analogous. To compare them and find their common ground let us look first at Christina Rossetti's poem.

Goblin Market tells the story of two sisters, Laura and Lizzie, and their encounters with the dangerous "other world" of goblins and spirits. Because they are both virgin-maids they hear "morning and evening… the goblin's cry: / 'Come buy our orchard fruits, / Come buy, come buy.'" They both know the sensual appetites that the goblins have and can 'infect' them with, and agree "We must not look at goblin men, / We must not buy their fruits: / Who knows upon what soil they fed / Their hungry thirsty roots?" One evening, however, hearing the goblins going by singing and carrying their fruit produce, Laura finds that she can no longer resist temptation: "They sounded kind and full of loves / In the pleasant weather." She buys fruit from them with a lock of her golden hair and sheds an irrepressible tear "more rare than pearl." Then "she sucked and sucked and sucked the more / Fruits which that unknown orchard bore; / She sucked until her lips were sore;..."

Transported by her sensual adventures (and the sexuality of her adventures doubtless, though it is not possible to say whether this occurred to Christina) she returns home to Lizzie who rebukes her. But Laura is addicted and determines to repeat her experience. Yet on the next evening she discovers to her dismay that she cannot hear the goblin's inviting cry, although Lizzie is able to since she has remained untouched. "Must she then buy no more such dainty fruit? / Must she no more such succous pasture find,... [She] gnashed her teeth for baulked desire, and wept / As if her heart would break."

This torture continues and she dwindled ("as the fair full moon doth turn / To swift decay and burn / Her fire away") only to be saved by Lizzie's noble self-sacrifice. For she determines to buy fruit for her from the goblins. But in the attempt, when it becomes clear to the goblins that she is not going to eat the fruit herself, their fury mounts and they feel that they have been cheated. Prevented from their seductive plan, they abuse her and virtually rape her with their sinful fruit:

> Lashing their tails
> They trod and hustled her,
> Elbowed and jostled her,
> Clawed with their nails,
> Barking, mewing, hissing, mocking,
> Tore her gown and soiled her stocking,
> Twitched her hair out by the roots,
> Stamped upon her tender feet,
> Held her hands and squeezed their fruits
> Against her mouth to make her eat.

She, of course, resists; a Pre-Raphaelite martyr to her cause:

> White and golden Lizzie stood,
> Like a lily in a flood;–...
> Like a beacon left alone
> In a hoary roaring sea,
> Sending up a golden fire;–...
> Like a royal virgin town
> Topped with gilded dome and spire
> Close beleaguered by a fleet
> Mad to tug her standard down.
>
> Lizzie uttered not a word;
> Would not open lip from lip
> Lest they should cram a mouthful in:
> But laughed in heart to feel the drip
> Of juice that syruped all her face,...

Badly beaten, she returns to her sister whom she tells to

> Come and kiss me.
> Never mind my bruises,
> Hug me, kiss me, suck my juices
> Squeezed from goblin fruits for you,
> Goblin pulp and goblin dew.
> Eat me, drink me, love me;...

Laura realizes what her sister has done for her and thinks that consequently they are now both doomed to a terrible fate ("Thirsty, cankered, goblin-ridden?...") and runs to comfort her, full of pity and with tears in her eyes. This selflessness reawakened in her is, of course, the antidote, though she has also to retaste the juice which crazed her in the first place. This time however "Swift fire spread through her veins, knocked at her heart, / Met the fire smoldering there / And overbore its lesser flame;..." She is thus eventually regenerated and the sisters become even more devoted to one another. Later both marry and warn their children of the danger of the goblins.

Carroll was right to admire this poem "very much" for it is, among all the rest of Christina's often somber verse, by far her most powerful poetic achievement. Whether or not she herself recognized that it is a poem that is highly charged with sexual motifs, this rape of the virgin is so blatant that one would have to be deliberately myopic not to recognize it as such. For here, the tensions between the love and fear of sex and the virtues of virginity, in contrast to the torment of sinful indulgence, tells us a great deal about Victorian sexuality and exposes all that dozens of polite novelettes of the period concealed. But whatever Christina thought she had written (and she does seem to have been a remarkably pure and innocent lady), Carroll, in his poem, certainly caught its tone. Carroll's poem, "Stolen Waters," which was written during precisely those "few days" around May 12th, 1862 when he was reading *Goblin Market*, also has its tempted virgin – but this time, appropriately enough, it is a man:

> The light was faint, and soft the air
> That breathed around the place;
> And she was lithe, and tall, and fair,
> And with a wayward grace
> Her queenly head she bare.
>
> With glowing cheek, with gleaming eye,
> She met me on the way:
> My spirit owned the witchery
> Within her smile that lay:
> I followed her, I know not why.

The trees were thick with many a fruit,
The grass with many a flower:
My soul was dead, my tongue was mute,
In that accursed hour.

And, in my dream, with silvery voice,
She said, or seemed to say,
Youth is the season to rejoice—'
I could not choose but stay;
I could not say her nay.

She plucked a branch above her head,
With rarest fruitage laden:
Drink of the juice, Sir Knight,' she said,
Tis good for knight and maiden.'

Oh, blind my eye that would not trace —
And, deaf mine ear that would not heed—
The mocking smile upon her face,
The mocking smile of greed!

I drank the juice, and straightway felt
A fire within my brain;
My soul within me seemed to melt
In sweet delirious pain.

'Sweet is the stolen draught,' she said;
'Hath sweetness stint or measure?
Pleasant the secret hoard of bread;
What bars us from our pleasure?'

Here is an encounter comparable to the one in *Goblin Market*; here, also, there is a dangerous conflict between innocent virtue and sinister, sinful sensuality. Moreover, the concept of the fruit, full of dangerous juice, is also substantially the same, as is the "fire" and the "sweet delirious pain" of indulgence. The subsequent events are also similar (although Carroll cannot tell them so well), except that the sexes are reversed. After his indulgence, like Laura's in *Goblin Market*, the Virgin-Hero of "Stolen Waters" begins to go into a rapid decline ("My happier life was dying") and his tempter, having taken over his heart, changes to the "withered, old and gray" being that she really was all the time. The Knight attempts to flee from her but "Still behind me seemed to hear / Her fierce unflagging tread; / And scarce drew breath for fear," and eventually contemplates suicide because, "The heart that once had been mine own… I bore instead / A cold, cold heart of stone." Luckily, however, whilst on his mournful travels he hears "a clear voice singing: / And suddenly, like summer rain, / My happy tears came springing: / My human heart returned again." The song that the Knight hears is about the trusting nature of childhood and "The simple joy of being:"

A rosy child—
Sitting and singing, in a garden fair,
The joy of hearing, seeing,
The simple joy of being—
Or twining rosebuds in the golden hair
That ripples free and wild.

A sweet pale child—
Wearily looking to the purple West—
Waiting for the great For-ever
That suddenly shall sever
The cruel chains that hold her from her rest—
By earth-joys unbeguiled....

Be as a child—
So shalt thou sing for very joy of breath—
So shalt thou wait thy dying,
In holy transport lying—
So pass rejoicing through the gate of death,
In garment undefiled.

The Knight's tears, like Laura's, bring him comfort and relief from the consequences of his indulgences and he wins back some of his serenity by recognizing that selflessness – as described in the song – is a quality that can compensate, in part at least, for his former willfulness. The final stanzas show, however, that unlike the maidens in *Goblin Market*, the Knight has suffered some permanent damage:

For if I weep, it is that now
I see how deep a loss is mine,
And feel how brightly round my brow
The coronal might shine,
Had I but kept mine early vow:

And if I smile, it is that now
I see the promise of the years—
That garland waiting for my brow,
That must be won with tears,
With pain—with death—I care not how.

The inevitable conclusion to be drawn from the similarities that exist between these poems is not merely that Carroll knew *Goblin Market*, but that he both subscribed and responded to the ideas expressed in it. It may seem astonishing to reflect that there were only eight weeks between the heavy writing of "Stolen Waters" and the first telling of *Alice* on that famous boat trip with Alice and her two sisters. Yet there is one vital link: as in *Goblin Market* and "Stolen Waters," so also in *Alice*, the notion of purity and pre-adulthood is preferred because the worlds of all three are potentially anarchic and damaging to the uninitiated, and this initiation, by its nature, means that though there are certain gains, the valuable quality of innocence is necessarily totally lost. Such initiation is a correlative to being attracted to what are seen as the miserable fruits of the adult world – according to these two chaste Victorians. Such pessimism – a direct result of inhibiting more fundamental sensual pleasures – was Carroll's view even more than Christina Rossetti's. For Laura and Lizzie recover and profit by their experience (though that remained sinful) and have a happy life with their children; Carroll's Knight (and the White Knight was his undoubted persona), on the other hand, gained nothing but heartache and melancholy, though he also gained the ability to appreciate the qualities of innocence and childhood that he had previously so willingly surrendered. The implication here is that to escape the goblins and witches of adulthood and their destructive sensuality, one must know something about them; to know something about them is already to be dangerously involved. To know that paradise can be lost is in itself to lose this particular kind of paradise – and not knowing that it is possible to lose it is only a matter of time:

> "Seven years and six months!" Humpty Dumpty repeated thoughtfully. "An uncomfortable sort of age. Now if you'd asked *my* advice, I'd have said 'Leave off at seven'—— but it's too late now."
> "I never ask advice about growing," Alice said indignantly.
> "Too proud?" the other enquired. Alice felt even more indignant at this suggestion. "I mean," she said, "that one can't help growing older."
> "*One* can't, perhaps," said Humpty Dumpty; "but *two* can. With proper assistance, you might have left off at seven."
> *Through the Looking-Glass*, Chapter VI

This bittersweet dilemma is always to be found in Carroll's work and it surely helps our understanding of *Alice* to know the deep feelings that are behind Carroll's apparently light touch. What is needed to stop growing old? If two are needed, who is the other one (a marriage partner?) Do we stop growing old by having our children to march on for us? All this is suddenly implied if the full weight of Carroll's serious ideology is kept in mind. His sensibility, like that of Christina Rossetti, was balanced between highly charged desire and fear, insecure and dangerous joy, all a prelude to inevitable and enduring wretched sin. Carroll's gloom pervades his *Diary*, and his life parallels hers in its chastity. Like her, he never seemed to come to happy adult maturity and its demands, but whereas she avoided it by looking to its conclusion, – that is, death – he looked backwards to the years of childhood. It is, however, more than coincidental that at times their worlds meet as in *Goblin Market* and "Stolen Waters" and that at other times they almost exchanged home territory; Christina writing nonsense verses in *Sing Song* and Carroll writing poems of death such as "Solitude" and "Only a Woman's Hair." It is important to recognize that the exquisite melancholy that is an obvious ingredient for Christina Rossetti in her work and for Carroll in these poems, and the *Sylvie and Bruno* volumes, is also present in the masterwork *Alice's Adventures in Wonderland*, and that it was a vital and contemporary Victorian source of artistic energy.

Carroll's friendship with Christina Rossetti demonstrates yet again that he was not an isolated eccentric Oxford don, but a fully subscribing member of the artistic community of his time.

ITEMS EXHIBITED

53) **Photograph of Christina Rossetti by Lewis Carroll.
October 6, 1863.**

Inscribed by Carroll in black ink: "Miss Christina Rossetti."
(See page 88 for illustration.)

54) a. **Photograph of Dante Gabriel Rossetti by Lewis Carroll.
October 6, 1863.**

b. **Photograph of Alexander Munro by Lewis Carroll.
October 7, 1863.**

The two photographs are from the George MacDonald family album.

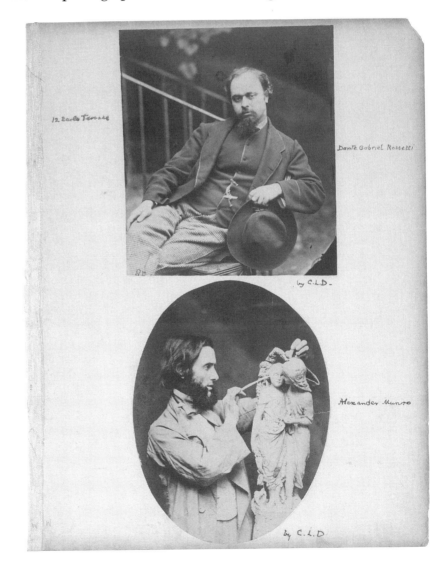

55) *SPEAKING LIKENESSES.* **By Christina Rossetti.**
   London: Macmillan, 1874.

Illustrated by Arthur Hughes in an *Alice*-like style. This book is often called the first parody of *Alice's Adventures in Wonderland*. The dust jacket is one of the earliest with an illustration.

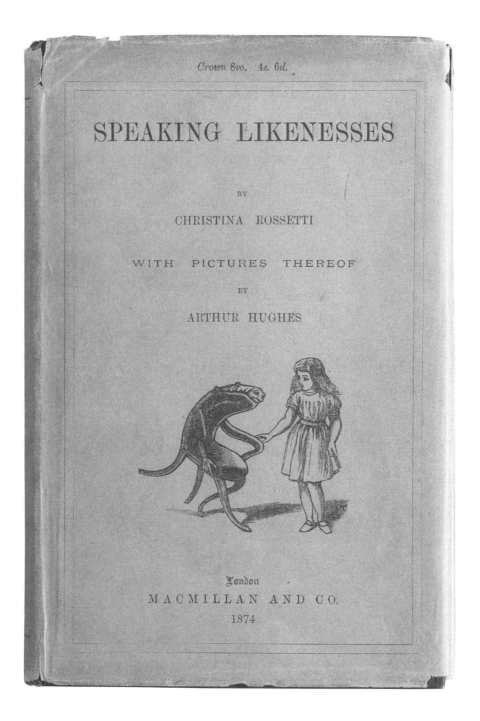

56) *TIME FLIES: A READING DIARY.* **By Christina G. Rossetti. London: Society for Promoting Christian Knowledge, 1885.**

Inscribed by Miss Rossetti in black ink on a white card pasted to the upper paste-down: "The Rev. C. L. Dodgson from C. G. R." Carroll had nine of her books in his library.

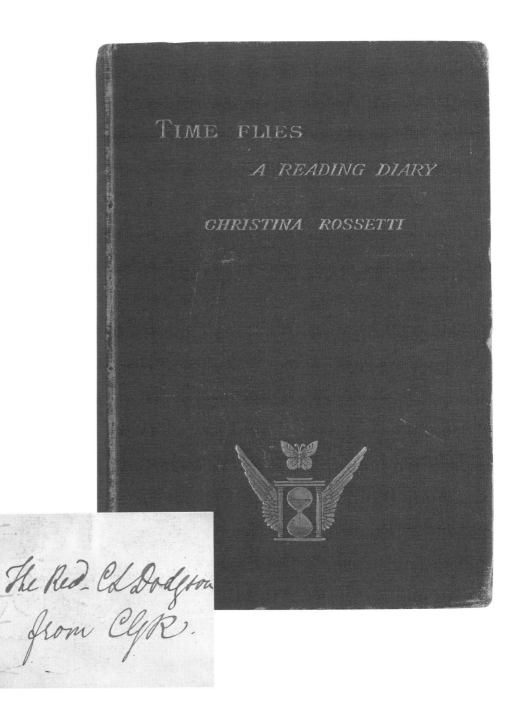

57) *ALICE'S ABENTEUER IM WUNDERLAND.* **von Lewis Carroll.
London: Macmillan, 1869.**

Inscribed by Carroll on the half-title in black ink: "Miss Christina Rossetti, with the Author's kind regards." This German edition of *Alice* is the first translation of the book into a foreign language.

Item 58

X
Charles L. Dodgson and the Theater

By Charles C. Lovett

Charles Dodgson was a man of many passions – mathematics, logic, children, photography, and the theater. In a time when the theater was emerging as a respectable entertainment, though still condemned by the Bishop of Oxford and other conservative churchmen, the Reverend Charles Dodgson was an enthusiastic, even obsessive, playgoer. Nearly every trip to London included an evening at a play, often accompanied by a friend, either child or adult. Dodgson attended his first performance in London in 1855, and his last in November of 1897, just two months before his death. It was written in one of his obituaries that "he had numerous acquaintances in the theatrical world of London, who respected his learning, humoured his amiable eccentricities, and keenly appreciated his wit." Dodgson loved to enter the various artistic "worlds" of Victorian England, cherishing his association with literary figures, painters, and, especially, members of the theatrical establishment. Actors, playwrights, and producers were all counted among Dodgson's friends.

While many still viewed the theater as immoral, Dodgson believed the stage could wield a positive influence on society. Certainly he included himself in the category of playgoer which he described as taking "an intelligent interest in plays, keenly enjoying all the good they find in them, and resenting with equal keenness all that is bad or even worthless." He was quick to condemn a play which he found immoral or irreverent, sometimes writing to the producer or lead actors of his opinion. A morally uplifting play he might view again and again, taking a string of young friends to share in the good he perceived. In his essay "The Stage and the Spirit of Reverence," Dodgson wrote of an ideal drama – the story of the Prodigal Son – in which, by the fourth act, "some eyes, even among the roughs of the Gallery [would] be 'wet with delicious tears,' and some hearts be filled with new and noble thoughts, and a spirit of 'reverence' be aroused."

Dodgson's love of the theater was intertwined with his love of children. He often took girls with him to see an appropriate play and he took a special interest in child actors, befriending them, introducing them to producers and actors, and defending them in the press when a movement was launched to ban children under ten from the stage. "Instead of being... miserable drudges who ought to be celebrated in a new 'Cry of the Children,'" wrote Dodgson of child actresses, "they simply *rejoice* in their work, 'even as a giant rejoiceth to run his course.'" As a result of lobbying by Dodgson and a group of theater professionals, the ban was modified, and children from seven to ten were still allowed to act. This must have brought great joy to the many stage children who were personal friends of "Lewis Carroll."

Given his passion for the theater and his talent for promoting his own works, it is not surprising that Dodgson turned his attention to the possibility of staging *Alice* shortly after the book was published. Dodgson approached several potential collaborators about this project over the years, including Thomas German Reed, producer of "dramatic entertainments with music," and Arthur Sullivan, composer of the music for the famous Gilbert and Sullivan operettas. Sadly, none of the contacts led to a collaboration, and we are left to wonder what a Carroll and Sullivan operetta might have been like.

Alice was staged as a private theatrical in 1874 and as an "entertainment" with music and dissolving views which ran for four months in 1877, but Dodgson was eager to see a full stage adaptation of his book. Finally, in 1886, he was approached by Henry Savile Clarke, a playwright, poet, writer of short stories, and editor of the newspaper *The Court Circular*. Savile Clarke wanted to adapt *Alice* and *Looking-Glass* into an operetta to be staged during the Christmas pantomime season in London. Dodgson wrote granting his permission on the condition that "neither in the libretto nor in any of the stage business, shall any coarseness, or anything suggestive of coarseness, be admitted."

Savile Clarke's *Alice in Wonderland, A Dream Play For Children, in Two Acts*, with music by Walter Slaughter, premiered at the Prince of Wales's Theatre on December 23, 1886 and ran in London through March 18, 1887, before beginning a successful provincial tour. The play was revived in 1888, when Alice was played by one of Dodgson's dearest child-friends, Isa Bowman. Though less successful than the original production, the revival still received complimentary notices in the London press.

ITEMS EXHIBITED

58) Poster Advertising Savile Clarke's *Alice in Wonderland*.

PRINCE OF WALES'S THEATRE ON THURSDAY AFTERNOON, DECEMBER 23, 1886, AND EVERY AFTERNOON, "ALICE IN WONDERLAND."

In his biography of his uncle, Stuart Dodgson Collingwood wrote, "Shortly before the production of the play, a Miss Whitehead had drawn a very clever medley-picture, in which nearly all Tenniel's wonderful creations appeared. This design was most useful as a 'poster' to advertise the play." Printed on thin paper, the poster was both bound in *The Court Circular* and used as a separate posted advertisement. In the bound volume of this periodical in The British Library, the poster appears between the December 17 and December 25 issues, and was probably originally included in the back of the December 17 issue. Very few copies have survived. (See page 102 for illustration.)

59) Playbill for Savile Clarke's *Alice in Wonderland* at the Prince of Wales's Theatre.

MR. EDGAR BRUCE'S MATINEES OF ALICE IN WONDERLAND
Every day at 2:30, Commencing On Thursday, December 23rd, 1886.

The Prince of Wales's Theatre was built as the Prince's Theatre in 1884 by Edgar Bruce and renamed in 1886. *Alice* was presented in this new theater under the glow of electric lighting. In the program, the playwright and poet, Henry Savile Clarke, paid tribute to Dodgson:

A Nursery Magician took
    All little children by the hand;
And led them laughing through the book,
    Where Alice walks in Wonderland,

Ours is the task with Elfin dance
    And song, to give to Childhood's gaze
That Wonderland; and should it chance
    To win a smile, be his the praise.

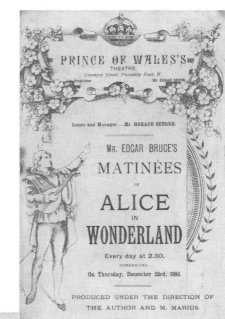

The fact that the cover illustration is unrelated to *Alice* is not surprising. Many London theaters of this period used the same design on the cover of every program, only altering the name of the play. *Alice in Wonderland* received largely positive notices. Though *The Court Circular*, which Savile Clarke edited, did not review the play, since it could hardly be impartial, it did run a weekly full-page advertisement which quoted from 20 different complimentary reviews.

60) *ALICE IN WONDERLAND*. A DREAM PLAY FOR CHILDREN, IN TWO ACTS. Founded upon Mr. Lewis Carroll's "Alice's Adventures in Wonderland," and "Through the Looking-Glass," With The Express Sanction Of The Author. By H. Savile Clarke. Music By Walter Slaughter. London: Published at "The Court Circular" Office, 1886.

The first edition of the script for Savile Clarke's play was rightly labeled "under revision" on the cover. Dodgson had kept up a steady stream of correspondence with Savile Clarke during the planning and rehearsing of the production, and while most of his suggestions were ignored by the playwright, a few were adopted. After the play opened, Dodgson felt that "The Walrus and the Carpenter" section did not have a suitable ending and he wrote some additional verses in which the ghosts of the oysters return seeking revenge. Subsequent printings of the play included these new verses, additional dialogue between Alice and the White Knight, and other revisions. The present version was published in December 1886; the new version was printed in early 1887. Not surprisingly, the script was published by *The Court Circular*, the newspaper edited by Savile Clarke. The script includes an advertisement for the "Christmas and Literary" number of *The Court Circular*, the only issue to which Lewis Carroll ever made a contribution–it includes a version of his word game "Mischmasch."

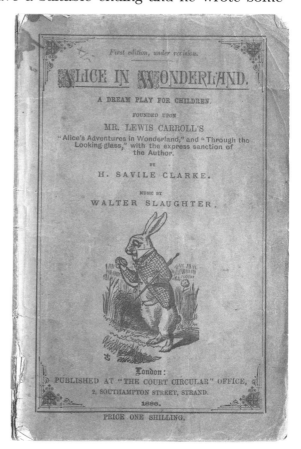

**61) Photograph, by an unknown photographer, of Phoebe Carlo
    as Alice in the 1886-87 production of Savile Clarke's
    *Alice in Wonderland.***

Dodgson himself first suggested Phoebe Carlo for the role of Alice, in a letter to Savile Clarke on October 26, 1886. He had first seen her on January 1, 1883 in *Whittington and his Cat* at the Avenue Theatre in London. Of her performance later that year as "Ned" in *The Silver King* (co-authored by one of Dodgson's favorite playwrights, Henry Arthur Jones), he wrote "Little Phoebe Carlo *looked* sweet, but had nothing to say." What a change the role of Alice must have been, where Miss Carlo had to carry every scene. One reviewer wrote that she was "safe and reliable in the part, and, by her acting, makes up for her not very good singing voice." Dodgson himself wrote, "Of Miss Phoebe Carlo's performance it would be difficult to speak too highly....What I admired most, as realizing most nearly my ideal heroine, was her perfect assumption of the high spirits, and readiness to enjoy *everything*, of a child out for a holiday."

Miss Phoebe Carlo.

62) *ALICE'S ADVENTURES IN WONDERLAND.* **By Lewis Carroll. London: Macmillan, 1886.**

Inscribed by Lewis Carroll in purple ink on the half-title:

> Presented to Violet Gordon by Lewis Carroll as a memento of her having taken part in the Dream-Play "Alice in Wonderland" written by H. Savile-Clarke and first produced Christmas, 1886.

On September 16, 1887, following the conclusion of the provincial tour of Savile Clarke's *Alice in Wonderland*, Dodgson wrote in his *Diary* that he went "To Macmillans', and inscribed 41 books to go to children who had acted in *Alice.*" Though only 13 children were credited in the original playbill for *Alice in Wonderland*, other children worked in the cast as the run wore on and as the play toured. In fact, when Dodgson saw the play in Brighton on July 14 he noted that it was "improved in cast." There is no record of what role Violet Gordon played.

63) *"'Alice' on the Stage."* **By Lewis Carroll.**
   THE THEATRE. A MONTHLY REVIEW OF THE DRAMA,
   MUSIC, AND THE FINE ARTS. **Edited By Clement Scott.**
   New Series, Vol. IX, April 1887, pp. 179-184.

Dodgson intended this article on the stage adaptation of his books to be the first in a series of articles to be published in *The Theatre.* A second article, "The Stage and the Spirit of Reverence," was published in June 1888, and a manuscript draft of an earlier article, "Dress," (dated November 11, 1885) survives, but there the series ended (though *The Theatre* did reprint Dodgson's letter to the *Sunday Times* on stage children in September 1889). This article includes Dodgson's own account of the genesis of the *Alice* stories and of *The Hunting of the Snark,* as well as a summary of his views on how the *Alice* characters ought to be interpreted dramatically. He writes with high praise of the Savile Clarke production, reserving special commendation for Sydney Harcourt, who played the Hatter and Tweedledum; Phoebe Carlo as Alice; and tiny Dorothy d'Alcourt, whose Dormouse was "the embodied essence of Sleep."

THE   THEATRE.

" Alice " on the Stage.

By Lewis Carroll.

" LOOK here; here's all this Judy's clothes falling to pieces again!" Such were the pensive words of Mr. Thomas Codlin; and they may fitly serve as motto for a writer who has set himself the unusual task of passing in review a set of puppets that are virtually his own—the stage-embodiments of his own dream-children.

Not that the play itself is in any sense mine. The arrangement, in dramatic form, of a story written without the slightest idea that it would ever be so adapted, was a task that demanded powers denied to me, but possessed in an eminent degree, so far as I can judge, by Mr. Savile Clarke. I do not feel myself qualified to criticise his play, as a play; nor shall I venture on any criticism of the players, as players.

What is it, then, that I have set myself to do? And what possible claim have I to be heard? My answer must be that, as the writer of the two stories thus adapted, and the originator (as I believe, for at least I have not *consciously* borrowed them) of the 'airy nothings' for which Mr. Savile Clarke has so skilfully provided, if not a name, at least a 'local habitation,' I may without

64) C. L. Dodgson to Mrs. Mallalieu (or whoever is in charge of Miss Polly Mallalieu). Autograph letter signed. October 20, 1891.

The letter is addressed "Dear Madam" and the envelope "Mrs Mallalieu (or whoever is in charge of Miss Polly Mallalieu)." Mary "Polly" Mallalieu was a child actress. The letter reads in part:

> though I have the pleasure of knowing a good many of the race of 'stage-children,' I should be very sorry to seem to <u>force</u> myself on the acquaintance of any... I signed myself to Polly, "yours affectionately," which, from an old gentlemen of nearly 60 to a child of 11, is not, I think, out of place: but, as she does not respond to that form of address, I do not write to her again, as I really cannot write to <u>children</u> on more formal terms.

Dodgson often saw young children on the stage and then befriended them, but as with his other attempts at child-friendships, while most succeeded, he was occasionally rebuffed. On October 10, 1891, Dodgson took two child-friends, the actress, Isa Bowman, and Gladys Baly, to see a production of *The Silver King* in Brighton. The role of Cissie, one of the children of Mr. and Mrs. Denver, was played by Polly Mallalieu, and Dodgson wrote to her the following day, explaining that whenever he saw *The Silver King* he always presented Cissie with an inscribed copy of one of his books. Presumably, Polly replied to his letter and told him which book she desired, for on October 17 he wrote her again, asking to know her home address so that he might call on her sometime. This request apparently led to the snub which prompted the present letter. Things were eventually smoothed over, though, and Dodgson met the Mallalieu family on June 25, 1892. A month later, he had Polly as his guest for a week at Guildford and Eastbourne.

The envelope for this letter.

Ch. Ch. Oxford
Oct. 20 /91

Dear Madam,

Whether I am addressing Polly's mother, or some one else who is in charge of her, I wish to say that, though I have the pleasure of knowing a good many of the race of "stage-children", I should be very sorry to seem to force myself on the acquaintance of any: &, if the fact that Polly merely tells me she does not live at Greenwich, without naming any home address, is to be taken to mean that it is not thought desirable that I should ever call (supposing I were ever near her home), I am quite content that it should be so.

I write this by return of post, as the best chance of its reaching you, as I know no other address than Northampton.

I signed myself, to Polly, "yours affectionately," which, from an old gentleman of nearly 60 to a child of 11, is not, I think, out of place: but, as she does not respond to that form of address, I do not write to her again, as I really can not write to children on more formal terms.

Believe me
    truly yours
        C L Dodgson.

Item 64

111

Item 67a   Upper wrapper for the "Twilight Version" of *Merryman's Monthly*.

XI
Lewis Carroll comes to America

By Selwyn H. Goodacre

It is a curious fact that the first works of Lewis Carroll to appear in the United States were either piracies, or rejected versions of English editions. The Lindseth Collection provides us with an unrivaled view of this bit of publishing history.

Nine years before the publication of *Alice's Adventures in Wonderland*, Lewis Carroll contributed one of his rare, humorous short stories, "Novelty and Romancement," to the English journal *The Train*, for the October 1856 issue. Sharp-eyed envoys for American publishers must have been delighted with this tale. It was exactly the sort of light-hearted material that could be republished in the States, without any trouble from the international copyright laws, which were then in an embryonic stage.

The story appeared, unattributed (which was the custom with pirated material), in the bound volume *The Harp of a Thousand Strings*, published by Dick & Fitzgerald of New York in 1858 [Item 65]. The book has been called "one of the most popular collections of humor of the 19th century." Even so, surviving copies are rare and the bibliography is complex, as all printings have the same title page and the same date. It would appear that Carroll was totally unaware that the piracy had ever occurred. In fact, it wasn't until 1930 that it was discovered that the book contained Lewis Carroll's story, his first literary appearance in America.

Carroll had a poor opinion of American standards of book publishing. In 1886 he rejected the first printing of *A Game of Logic*, commenting, "They will do very well for the Americans, who ought not to be very particular as to *quality*, as they insist on having books so very cheap." In his *Diary*, he put it even more bluntly, commenting that he had asked Macmillan to "send these 500 to America – just what happened in '65 with *Alice*, when the first 2000,... turned out so bad that I condemned them to the same fate." He was to do it again in 1889 with *The Nursery "Alice."*

The story of the rejection of the 1865 edition of *Alice* is discussed in my essay in this catalogue, "The 1865 *Alice*." Some of the details of how the rejected sheets were sold to the firm of D. Appleton and Co. of New York are less well known.

William Worthen Appleton, grandson of the founder, Daniel Appleton, was on a buying trip to London in April 1866. He was 21 years old, and it was his decision to purchase the unbound sheets of *Alice* for publication in America.

He negotiated the deal with George Lillie Craik of Macmillan's. A new title page was needed. Carroll was charged for "1000 titles to *Alice*, American Edition." These cancel title pages were printed in duplicate and the two differ slightly. In one, the B in By is directly above the T in Tenniel, and in the other, it is above and just to the right of the T. In my essay, "The 1865 *Alice*," I discuss

ALICE'S

ADVENTURES IN WONDERLAND.

BY

LEWIS CARROLL,

WITH FORTY-TWO ILLUSTRATIONS

BY

JOHN TENNIEL.

BY

JOHN TENNIEL.

NEW YORK

D. APPLETON AND CO., 445, BROADWAY.

1866.

Variant 1 of the Appleton *Alice* title page.

the two variants of that book. With two variants of the 1865 sheets, (in the second preliminary [b²]), and two variants of the cancel title page, there are four possible variants of the Appleton *Alice*, all of which are in the Lindseth Collection [Item 66 is one of these].

The cancel title page was mounted on the stub of the old one, the sheets machine folded and bound in cloth boards almost identical to the original English binding, apart from Appleton's name at the foot of the spine. Unlike the 1865 *Alice* (but like the new English 1866 edition), the edges were gilded.

The Appleton *Alice* initially did not sell well, and William Appleton found himself called upon more than once to defend his decision, and, indeed, had

ALICE'S

ADVENTURES IN WONDERLAND.

BY

LEWIS CARROLL.

WITH FORTY-TWO ILLUSTRATIONS

BY

JOHN TENNIEL.

BY

JOHN TENNIEL.

NEW YORK

D. APPLETON AND CO., 445, BROADWAY.

1866.

Variant 2 of the Appleton *Alice* title page.

to submit to a good deal of jesting at his expense. Copies are said to have lain in the Appleton stockroom in practically untouched piles for some months. Then, all of a sudden, the stock of books seemed to "melt away." *Alice* had "arrived" in America.

It would be some time before there were to be any further book editions of *Alice*. This gap was filled by Jesse Haney and his three piracies, which are displayed together here for the first time.

Jesse Haney was something of a nineteenth-century magazine entrepreneur and his name is associated with many periodicals. To publish *Alice* he simply "lifted" the text wholesale from the Appleton edition and printed it in three of his magazines and journals.

Lewis Carroll wrote to Macmillan on January 5, 1867 that he had received from America "*Merryman's Monthly* for December, in which they have actually reprinted half the book and copied about a dozen of the pictures! ending with 'Conclusion next month.'" In fact, the first half of *Alice* appeared in the January 1867 issue, and the second half in the February 1867 issue. In a notice on page 31 of the magazine, Haney states that it would be issued "in time to reach all but the most distant points by the fifteenth of the month preceding its date," thus accounting for Carroll's confusion with the December date. The story is printed in double columns, missing the concluding section about Alice's sister, and only including 19 of the 42 Tenniel pictures.

However, Haney also issued *Merryman's Monthly* in the form of a paper wrappered "book," the wrapper being titled *Fun For All! A Collection of Mirthful Morsels for Merry Moments. Served up by Mr. Merryman, who nose he nose how* with the publisher being noted as The American News Company, New York. They were "General Agents" for Haney. The "book" includes the two issues of *Merryman's Monthly*, each printing half of *Alice*, though there is no mention of *Alice* on the wrappers. Books of this type came to be called "twilight books." The Lindseth copy is the only known survivor [Item 67a].

Haney next pirated *Alice* in *The Children's Library* [Item 67b]. The entire text appears in one issue of over 30 pages – three columns to a page, again omitting the final five paragraphs, and with the same 19 Tenniel pictures. Though undated, it is possible to make an educated guess as to when it was published. An article in the journal mentions the sale "a few months ago" of a copy of the Eliot Indian Bible. The Bruce copy was sold in April 1868. An advertisement shows an adding machine with the patent date of March 10, 1868 clearly visible. All this suggests a publishing date of around June or July 1868. Only one copy is known. It is in the Berg Collection in The New York Public Library.

Haney's third piracy was in his *Haney's Journal* in 1869 [Item 67c]. This time *Alice* appeared in eight monthly parts from March to October 1869 (Vol. 2, Nos. 15-22). The text is again in three columns to the page, with the same exclusions and the same 19 Tenniel pictures, and is probably from the same type set up as *The Children's Library*.

Back in England, *Alice* was rapidly becoming a best seller. Such success could not be ignored, and there were soon plans to publish it in book form entirely in America.

Lee and Shepard of Boston were the first off the mark with their publication of *Alice* in 1869 [Item 68]. They based the text and layout on the Appleton *Alice*, but some of the smaller pictures were moved, and they made some odd changes to the Tenniel pictures. The picture of the giant puppy has the top corners of the border rounded off. In the picture of the Cheshire Cat at the Croquet Game, the corners are angled. The borders are removed entirely in the picture of the Gryphon and Mock Turtle.

The book binding was based on the original English design, but in a rather coarser cloth. The production was obviously a success, as reprints followed rapidly, starting in 1870. In 1871 they added the dual imprint of Lee and Shepard in Boston, and Lee, Shepard, and Dillingham in New York. The 1872 reprint is known in a whole host of binding variants. One is tempted to wonder if this sudden flowering had anything to do with the appearance of *Through the Looking-Glass*, first published that year.

Further reprints of the Lee and Shepard *Alice* followed in 1874, 1875, and 1876, after which they abruptly abandoned the book, leaving the field clear for the New York branch of Macmillan's to take over.

The story of the American publication of *Through the Looking-Glass* in 1872 has only recently become clear. In 1984, the Carroll scholar Hilda Bohem said there was a strong likelihood that the Lee and Shepard, 1872 American first edition [Item 69], predated the English first edition. Lee and Shepard made arrangements to purchase the book directly from Macmillan in London, who wrote in a letter that "the shipment now made is considerably in advance of both those we are to send to our house in New York and of the English publication...."

This must mean that the Lee and Shepard, the New York Macmillan, and the London Macmillan issues are all separate issues of the first edition – and it would seem that Lee and Shepard has the priority.

ITEMS EXHIBITED

65) *"Novelty and Romancement."* **By Lewis Carroll.**
THE HARP OF A THOUSAND STRINGS.
New York: Dick & Fitzgerald, 1858.

This pirated and unattributed story was Lewis Carroll's first literary appearance in America.

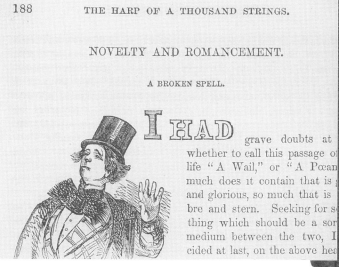

66) *ALICE'S ADVENTURES IN WONDERLAND.* **By Lewis Carroll. New York: D. Appleton and Co., 1866.**

The first American edition of *Alice's Adventures in Wonderland* was published using the suppressed 1865 sheets with a cancel title page. There are four variants, all of which are in the Lindseth Collection. (See pages 114 and 115 for illustrations.)

67) THREE JESSE HANEY PIRACIES OF *ALICE'S ADVENTURES IN WONDERLAND.* **Exhibited here for the first time.**

    a) *FUN FOR ALL! A COLLECTION OF MIRTHFUL MORSELS FOR MERRY MOMENTS. Served up by MR. MERRYMAN, who nose he nose how.* **New York: American News Company, (1867).**

Includes a wrapper (see page 112 for illustration) and the January and February 1867 issues of *Merryman's Monthly*, both in their original wrappers. Each of the two issues of *Merryman's* includes half of *Alice*. This is called a "twilight book" and is the only known copy in this form. Known also are two bound sets of the 1867 run of *Merryman's*. This is Jesse Haney's first piracy of *Alice.*

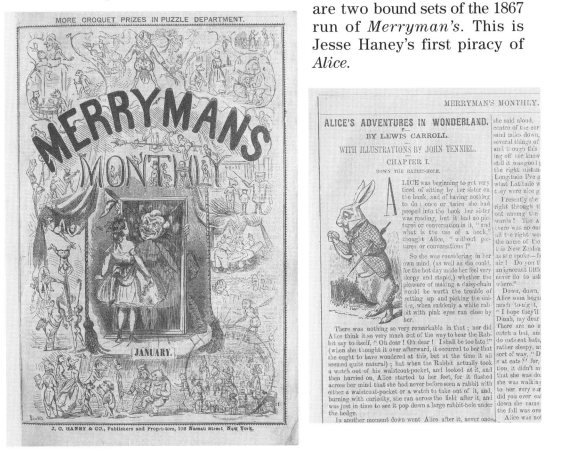

b) *THE CHILDREN'S LIBRARY.* **Vol. 1. Number one—complete. New York: Jesse Haney & Co., (1868).**

Jesse Haney's second pirated printing of *Alice*. This is the only known copy, and is from the Berg Collection in The New York Public Library. They have kindly loaned it for this exhibition.

Illustrations of *The Children's Library* reproduced by permission of The New York Public Library.

c) *HANEY'S JOURNAL.* New York: Jesse Haney & Co. Vol. II. Nos. 15-22. March - October 1869.

Haney's third piracy of *Alice* was printed in eight monthly parts. There are eight copies known of this journal and this is the only example, unbound, still in original parts. Two of the parts are partly unopened.

68) *ALICE'S ADVENTURES IN WONDERLAND.* **By Lewis Carroll.**
Boston: Lee and Shepard, 1869.

The first edition of *Alice* printed in America (except for the Haney piracies). Six printings are in the Lindseth Collection in fourteen binding variants.

69) *THROUGH THE LOOKING-GLASS.* **By Lewis Carroll.**
Boston: Lee and Shepard. New York: Lee, Shepard and Dillingham, 1872.

The first publication in America of *Through the Looking-Glass*. It is now thought that this edition predates both the Macmillan editions of London and New York and, therefore, has priority. Four binding variants are in the Lindseth Collection.

THROUGH THE LOOKING-GLASS,

AND WHAT ALICE FOUND THERE.

BY
LEWIS CARROLL,
AUTHOR OF "ALICE'S ADVENTURES IN WONDERLAND."

WITH FIFTY ILLUSTRATIONS
BY JOHN TENNIEL.

Boston:
LEE AND SHEPARD.
New York:
LEE, SHEPARD, AND DILLINGHAM.
1872.

[*The Right of Translation and Reproduction is reserved.*]

Item 70   Upper cover of the Nabokov Russian translation of *Alice*.

XII
Alice in Translation

By Jon A. Lindseth

Lewis Carroll was eager to have *Alice's Adventures in Wonderland* translated into other languages. In a letter to Alexander Macmillan of August 24, 1866, he wrote, "I should be glad to know what you think of my idea of putting it into French, or German, or both, and trying for a Continental sale." And in another letter to Macmillan, this one dated October 24, 1866, Carroll wrote that, "Friends here seem to think that the book is *untranslatable* into either French or German: the puns and songs being the chief obstacle." Carroll must have felt that the obstacle could be overcome because by April 1867, he had engaged translators for both editions.

Despite Carroll's enthusiasm, it was 1869 before the book appeared in translation, first the German, then the French. These were quickly followed by a Swedish edition in 1870, an Italian in 1872, both Dutch and Danish in 1875, Russian in 1879, and even one chapter in shorthand in 1889. By the time of Carroll's death in 1898, the book had been translated into seven languages – a substantial number but only a small percentage of those that were to follow.

Many claims are made on behalf of the "most popular children's story." A typical example appeared in the June 1996 issue of *The Magazine Antiques* where the author of an article on Beatrix Potter informed us that *The Tale of Peter Rabbit* has been "translated into more than a dozen languages, from Afrikaans to Japanese," and that, therefore, "it may well be the most popular children's story of all time." But, if the number of languages in translation is a fair test of popularity, *Peter Rabbit* falls far short of *Alice's Adventures in Wonderland* which has been translated into 75 languages, according to my count, 67 of which are represented in my collection.

A great deal has been written about the popularity of *Alice* in translation. In Japan, for instance, there are currently 60 different editions in print. One edition, first published in 1952, reached its thirty-third printing in 1991. Nina Demourova, in her article "Alice Speaks Russian" published in the winter 1994-95 issue of the *Harvard Library Bulletin*, quotes the late Russian mathematician and *Alice* collector, Alexander Roushaylo, who wrote: "*Alice* has been published in the Soviet Union more than seventy times in eleven languages, including English, with print runs exceeding six million copies." Total translations of *Alice* in all languages amount to 1,978 editions and printings, according to Joel Birenbaum, President of the Lewis Carroll Society of North America, who maintains this census. And as of this writing, Schoenhof's Foreign Books of Cambridge, Massachusetts, had in stock 33 editions in 16 different languages.

Part of the reason for the enormous popularity of *Alice* was noted by

Warren Weaver in his 1964 book *Alice in Many Tongues*, the first census of *Alice* translations. (At that time, he was able to identify 43 different languages.) Weaver said, "*Alice in Wonderland* is, in effect, two books: a book for children and a book for adults." Carroll would have liked that explanation and might have responded by saying, "a book is what you want it to be, nothing more, nothing less."

ITEM EXHIBITED

70) *ANYA V STRANE CHUDES*. [ANYA IN WONDERLAND]. Berlin: Izdatel'stvo Ganayun, 1923. Translated by V. Sirin (Pseudonym of Vladimir Nabokov). Illustrated by S. V. Zalshupin.

Спустя нѣсколько минутъ ходьбы они увидѣли вдали Чепупаху, которая сидѣла грустная и одинокая на небольшой скалѣ. А приблизившись, Аня разслышала ея глубокіе, душу раздирающіе вздохи. Ей стало очень жаль ее.

83

Nabokov was a student at Cambridge University at the time and was reported to have been paid £5 to translate *Alice* into Russian. Nina Demourova, in her article in the *Harvard Library Bulletin*, wrote, "Nabokov's translation stands out from the early translations. It is vigorous and has a degree of freedom that bespeaks a future master."

The illustrations for this book are by S. V. Zalshupin, clearly influenced by the Russian Constructivists, who were among the world's leading graphic artists in the early twentieth century. Many of the Russian artists emigrated to Berlin both before and after the 1917 Revolution.

Two copies of this book are displayed. One in boards, showing the cover, and a second in wrappers, showing the illustration on page 83. Since the paper of this period is very acidic, both copies have had the staples removed and the paper deacidified.

THE LEWIS CARROLL SOCIETY

If you would like more information on Lewis Carroll or would like to join one of the Lewis Carroll Societies in America, England, Japan or Canada, please write:

- **_In America:_** Contact Ellie Luchinsky, Secretary, The Lewis Carroll Society of North America, 18 Fitzharding Place, Owing Mills, MD 21117. The Society publishes a newsletter and maintains a home page on the Internet.

  The Lewis Carroll Society of North America Home Page at: http://www.lewiscarroll.org

- **_In England:_** Contact Sarah Stanfield, Secretary, The Lewis Carroll Society, Acorns, Dargate, Near Faversham, Kent ME13 9HG England. The Society publishes a journal of scholarly articles twice a year, a newsletter, a journal of reviews of Carroll related books, and maintains a home page on the Internet.

  The Lewis Carroll Society Home Page at: http://ourworld.compuserve.com/homepages/Aztec/LCS.htm

- **_In Japan:_** Contact Katsuko Kasai, Secretary, The Lewis Carroll Society of Japan, 3-6-15 Funato, Abiko-Shi, Chiba 270-11, Japan. The Society publishes a newsletter and a journal.

- **_In Canada:_** Contact Dayna McCausland, The Lewis Carroll Society of Canada, Box 321, Erin, Ontario, Canada N0B 1TO.

NOTES ON CONTRIBUTORS

Francine F. Abeles is Professor of Mathematics and Computer Science at Kean University of New Jersey. She is editor of *The Mathematical Pamphlets of Charles Dodgson and Related Pieces* and has written extensively on Dodgson's mathematical work and his pamphlets on voting.

Morton N. Cohen is the author of *Lewis Carroll, A Biography* and editor of *The Letters of Lewis Carroll*. He has written numerous articles and books on Carroll and is a popular speaker at Carroll conferences. He is Professor Emeritus of the City University of New York and a Fellow of the Royal Society of Literature, London.

Rodney Engen is the author of fifteen books in the field of Victorian art and illustration. Among his books are *Sir John Tenniel, Alice's White Knight* and *A Dictionary of Victorian Wood Engravers*. In addition, he writes for newspapers and magazines. He lives in Whistler's house in London.

Selwyn H. Goodacre specializes in the bibliographical aspects of Carroll's work and is compiling a handbook of Carroll's writing. He is past chairman of the Lewis Carroll Society (England) and former editor of *Jabberwocky, the Journal of the Lewis Carroll Society*.

Edward Guiliano has written and edited many books on Lewis Carroll and is currently a series editor of *The Pamphlets of Lewis Carroll*. He is Vice President of Academic Affairs at the New York Institute of Technology. His special interest is Victorian literature.

Charles C. Lovett is a past president of The Lewis Carroll Society of North America and author of *Alice on Stage*, which he is now revising for the second edition. He is co-author of the bibliography *Lewis Carroll's Alice*. He is currently a series editor of *The Pamphlets of Lewis Carroll*.

Jeffrey Stern is an antiquarian bookseller in York, England, specializing in the history of education and enterprise. His doctoral dissertation was on Lewis Carroll about whom he continues to write extensively. In 1997 he published the second of his books on Carroll's library, *Lewis Carroll, Bibliophile*.

Edward Wakeling is a former chairman of the Lewis Carroll Society (England) and has an M.Sc. from Carroll's college, Christ Church, Oxford. He has written or edited a number of books on Carroll and is now editing an edition of *Lewis Carroll's Diaries*. He is working on a catalogue raisonné of Carroll's photographs.

OF THIS CATALOGUE 1400 COPIES HAVE BEEN PRINTED
OF WHICH 42 NUMBERED COPIES ARE BOUND IN
CLOTH-COVERED BOARDS

One may reasonably ask why there are 42 numbered copies of this catalogue. The answer is, Lewis Carroll was fascinated with this number, which was certainly his favorite. The number appears many times in his writing. There are 42 illustrations in *Alice's Adventures in Wonderland* and this fact is printed on the title page. In the trial scene of *Alice*, the King "called out 'Silence' and read out from his book, 'Rule Forty-two. All persons more than a mile high to leave the court.'" In the Preface to *The Hunting of the Snark*, Carroll cites another Rule 42, this one from the Naval Code, "No one shall speak to the Man at the Helm." Also in *Snark*, the Baker has 42 boxes of belongings, and in one illustration the box numbered 42 is clearly seen. These are just a few examples of Carroll's frequent use of this number. We can only surmise why Carroll was so taken by the number 42 as there is no manuscript or printed work in which he explained his fascination.

For more information on the number 42 and Lewis Carroll see: "What I tell you Forty-Two Times is True!" by Edward Wakeling in *Jabberwocky, The Journal of the Lewis Carroll Society*, Autumn 1977, Vol. 6, No. 4, (issue no. 32), pp. 101-106.

PRINTED IN THE UNITED STATES OF AMERICA IN 1998

BY WATT PRINTERS

PHOTOGRAPHY BY WETZLER STUDIOS

DESIGNED BY TOM LADYGA